Jennifer Anderson

The Limits of Sino-Russian Strategic Partnership

Adelphi Paper 315

Oxford University Press, Great Clarendon Street, Oxford OX2 6DP
Oxford New York
Athens Auckland Bangkok Bombay Calcutta Cape Town
Dar es Salaam Delhi Florence Hong Kong Istanbul Karachi
Kuala Lumpur Madras Madrid Melbourne Mexico City
Nairobi Paris Singapore Taipei Tokyo Toronto
and associated companies in
Berlin Ibadan

Oxford is a trade mark of Oxford University Press

Published in the United States
by Oxford University Press Inc., New York

© The International Institute for Strategic Studies 1997

First published December 1997 by **Oxford University Press** for
The International Institute for Strategic Studies
23 Tavistock Street, London WC2E 7NQ

Director John Chipman
Editor Gerald Segal
Assistant Editor Matthew Foley
Design and Production Mark Taylor

British Library Cataloguing in Publication Data
Data available

Library of Congress Cataloguing in Publication Data

ISBN 0-19-829427-1
ISSN 0567-932X

contents

Since the nineteenth century, relations between Russia and China have been constrained by competition, mutual suspicion and enduring cultural differences. The Sino-Soviet split in the early 1960s added an ideological dimension to these divisions and led to a massive military build-up along the two countries' 4,300-kilometre border. Tensions eased with the formal normalisation of relations in 1989 and the end of the Cold War, but few observers expected mutual distrust to end.

Yet within a year of the Soviet Union's collapse in 1991, Russia began to court China anew. By 1996, the two countries had forged an apparently fresh relationship – a so-called 'strategic partnership' – based on shared domestic and international concerns. Summits have been held, wide-ranging joint statements issued and well over 100 agreements initialled, including confidence-building and demilitarisation treaties covering the former Sino-Soviet border. Plans have been aired to increase bilateral trade to $20 billion by 2000. Beijing and Moscow claim this emerging partnership as the foundation for a new security mechanism in the Asia-Pacific region and, eventually, a new international order.

However, the substance of the relationship belies its rhetoric. China's rise as an East Asian power prompts fears in Russia about Beijing's long-term intentions; cross-border ties remain fraught, mutual suspicions high and cultural differences stark. Two-way trade has proved volatile and will almost certainly not reach its declared target by 2000. Elements in Russia have resisted border

Map I *The Russian Federation and China*

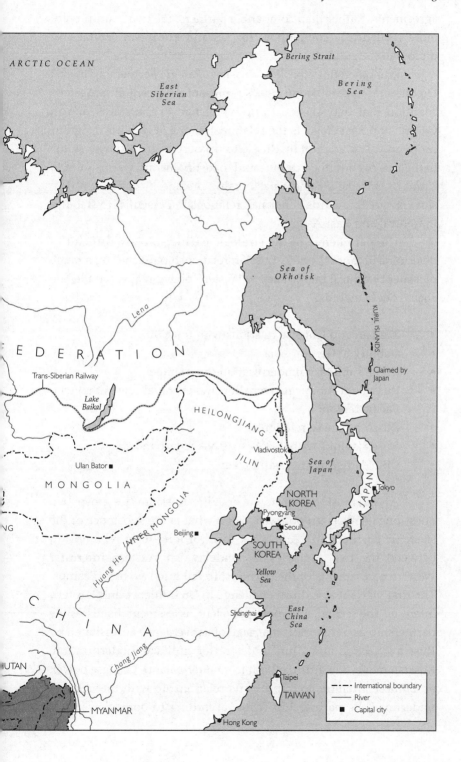

ARCTIC OCEAN

East
Siberian
Sea

Bering Strait

Bering
Sea

Sea of
Okhotsk

Lena

EDERATION

Trans-Siberian Railway

Lake
Baikal

HEILONGJIANG

KURIL ISLANDS

Claimed by
Japan

Vladivostok

JILIN

Sea of
Japan

JAPAN

Tokyo

Ulan Bator ■

NORTH
KOREA

MONGOLIA

Pyongyang

Seoul

NG

INNER MONGOLIA

Beijing ■

SOUTH
KOREA

Huang He

Yellow
Sea

C H I N A

Shanghai

East
China
Sea

Chang Jiang

HUTAN

Taipei

TAIWAN

MYANMAR

Hong Kong

International boundary
River
■ Capital city

agreements. Rather than compatible partners, the two countries are more realistically competitors for US and European capital and diplomatic attention.

What then does the Sino-Russian strategic partnership mean? Do bilateral ties in the late 1990s represent a nascent anti-Western coalition that may pose a future challenge to the status quo in Central and East Asia? Is the relationship one of rhetorical significance only – an attempt by Russia to reassert its great-power status in the face of continued decline and to justify lucrative arms sales to China? Or is the strategic partnership a stage in both countries' slow progress towards a 'normal' relationship, essential to stability in Central and East Asia?

The parameters of the strategic partnership are difficult to determine because the Sino-Russian relationship touches on a range of issues of central importance to Western policy-makers in the late 1990s. These include:

- Russian and Chinese relations with the US;
- stability in Central Asia;
- China's military-modernisation programme;
- Russia's economic rejuvenation and eventual role in the Asia-Pacific region;
- Russo-Japanese relations;
- Russia's links with the West as NATO expands; and
- China's rise as an Asian power.

At its most basic, however, Sino-Russian ties pose two questions for Western policy-makers: what is the substance of the strategic partnership? And what form of long-term relationship between the two countries is conducive to Western interests? Western assessments of the partnership fall into two broad camps. The first views it as a direct challenge to US influence and Western interests. The second, and more prevalent, assessment dismisses the partnership as a rhetorical marriage of convenience necessitated by Russia's decline and China's desire for military modernisation. Russian moves towards the West to counter-balance Chinese power, or Chinese attempts to improve its relationship with the US, will undermine the partnership. Thus, according to both views, promoting positive Sino-Russian relations should not be an explicit policy goal. Continued mutual distrust is useful in that it limits Russian arms sales to China and ensures that neither country can rely on a stable mainland flank as a basis for a more assertive stance in Maritime or Central Asia.

This paper takes a step back from both perspectives. It argues that the Sino-Russian strategic partnership is best understood as overlaying a distinct, and at times contradictory, diplomatic agenda established by Soviet leader Mikhail Gorbachev in the late 1980s. This project aimed to end the Sino-Soviet conflict by normalising bilateral relations. Partnership shares normalisation's goals of economic cooperation and cross-border stability, but differs in its overriding concern to manage relations at an élite political level, rather than to establish a strong and open relationship. Since 1991, Russia has sought to create similar strategic or constructive partnerships with Western countries such as the US and Germany and with South Korea. More recently, Moscow has sought partnerships with India and Iran as counter-weights to US influence and as vehicles to promote Russian economic interests in Central and East Asia.

Figures within Russian President Boris Yeltsin's government have seen China as a strategic counterpoise to the West and NATO, but an overtly anti-Western relationship has not materialised. China's approach is pragmatic and limited; any form of strategic partnership would run counter to fundamental tenets of modern Chinese foreign policy. Moreover, Beijing has maintained an unsentimental view of Russia's economic prospects, frustrating Moscow's attempts to use political progress to win major Chinese contracts and investment. For its part, Yeltsin's government is hampered by limited domestic support for economic and political reform, competing private interests, each with a stake in government policy, and a tendency to view partnership as a means of side-stepping normalisation.

As a result, Russia and China's relationship in the late 1990s is uneven, largely rhetorical and élite-driven, complicating the still-incomplete normalisation process. Both countries understand the risks of returning to outright confrontation, but, despite statements to the contrary, a 'normal' relationship has yet to be established.

Insofar as a partnership exists, it is a modest commitment to mutual non-interference and recognition of respective strategic interests in Central and East Asia. Aspects of the relationship, notably Russian arms sales, are cause for Western concern. However, the greatest immediate dangers are that Russia risks placing a largely rhetorical strategic partnership above substantive normalisation, and that Western analysts, concerned by China's possible long-term intentions in Asia, no longer see a stable and open Sino-Russian relationship as an important element in strategic stability.

chapter 1

Normalisation and Partnership

The Russian–Chinese strategic partnership was grafted onto a framework to normalise bilateral relations – based on border-demarcation and demilitarisation talks and enhanced trade ties – established by Gorbachev and Chinese paramount leader Deng Xiaoping in the 1980s. Following the collapse of the Soviet Union, Yeltsin moved quickly to affirm Russia's commitment to this framework and has deviated little from Gorbachev's negotiating positions. However, the political importance to Russia of its relations with China has increased significantly: within a year of taking power, the Yeltsin government began to court China as its preferred partner in Asia and, more broadly, as a diplomatic ally. This ambitious partnership agenda has been pursued in tandem with, but distinct from, the pragmatic and cautious normalisation process established by Gorbachev.

Normalisation
Deng's call in 1989 for 'ending the past, opening up the future' encapsulated early Soviet and Chinese efforts to establish a stable bilateral relationship.[1] The Sino-Soviet split of the mid-1960s had, by the late 1980s, resulted in Chinese claims to 35,000 square kilometres of Soviet land in the Far East and Central Asia, and Soviet economic, political and strategic isolation. The lengthy Sino-Soviet border had become one of the most heavily militarised in the world.[2] Between 1965 and 1985, the number of Soviet ground forces in the Far East,

Siberia and Central Asia grew from 170,000 troops to some 500,000, backed by conventional and nuclear air and missile forces and the Soviet Pacific Fleet.[3] This military build-up, however, damaged the Soviet Union both economically and strategically. The split with China opened a second front in the West's confrontation with the Soviet Union that was exploited by both Beijing and Washington throughout the 1970s and 1980s. Links that the Soviet Far East had maintained across the Chinese border were severed.[4] By the late 1970s, China's trading relationships had shifted southwards and across the Pacific, leaving the Soviet Far East increasingly isolated from the dynamic development of the Asia-Pacific region.

By the early 1980s, the Soviet leadership recognised that normalising relations with China was key to reducing its military burden and exploiting its vast Far Eastern resources. Cross-border trade and border-demarcation talks were revived in 1982, just before then Soviet leader Leonid Brezhnev's death, although it was Gorbachev who moved decisively to reduce Sino-Soviet competition and to resolve border tensions. In a speech in Vladivostok in July 1986, Gorbachev addressed China's three preconditions for normalising relations: he announced troop reductions in Afghanistan and Mongolia; voiced support for normalised Sino-Vietnamese relations; and agreed to settle disputed river boundaries between the Soviet Far East and northern China in accordance with international law. Beijing responded by dropping references to Soviet 'ideological revisionism' and to the Soviet 'threat' from official discourse, and revised its military doctrine accordingly.[5] By October 1986, the two sides had agreed to discuss the situation in Cambodia, and, in April 1989, Vietnam announced that it would withdraw all its forces from Cambodia by that September. In May 1989, Gorbachev visited Beijing, re-establishing ties and advancing border and demilitarisation negotiations. Then Soviet Foreign Minister Eduard Shevardnadze announced that 250,000 troops would be removed from the Far East, including 120,000 directly facing China. Gorbachev proposed complete demilitarisation along the Sino-Soviet border, opening the way for a meeting later in 1989 which began to negotiate a demilitarised zone. In 1991, the two powers signed an agreement outlining demarcation principles for their disputed eastern border. A final 1991 Sino-Soviet Joint Communiqué included an 'anti-hegemony' provision which, in the view of most analysts, marked the end of the Cold War struggle to dominate the regional balance of power.

The collapse of the Soviet Union removed most of the factors that had complicated bilateral relations. Neither post-Soviet Russia nor China viewed the other as a serious military threat; with the end of the Cold War, Beijing saw no strategic benefits in pursuing bilateral ties with Russia in the context of its relations with the US. At the same time, neither Russia nor China saw a strong bilateral political relationship taking shape. The Chinese leadership had openly courted Soviet conservatives at Yeltsin's expense in the last months of Soviet power, and cited Russia's economic collapse as vindicating Beijing's economic reforms. China embarked on a new wave of coastal economic development following Deng's 'Southern Tour' in 1992 that reinforced the economic importance of the coastal south. Russia courted the US and Japan and openly challenged Beijing over its human-rights record.

fast-paced, pragmatic relations

Nevertheless, both Beijing and Moscow continued to focus on establishing a stable bilateral relationship conducive to their internal-reform programmes. China recognised the Russian Federation on 27 December 1991 and emphasised its willingness to fulfil the treaties it had signed with the former Soviet government. On 31 January 1992, Yeltsin pledged to respect the 1991 agreement on demarcation principles. The Supreme Soviet ratified the agreement on 13 February 1992, and further economic and border negotiations resumed the following month. Cross-border trade grew, helped by the introduction of visa-free travel, and Russia and China seemed to have created a modest, process-driven arrangement conforming to Deng's 1989 injunction to forgo ideology in favour of concrete achievements.

Ties with Russia were part of China's 'good neighbour' diplomacy designed to lessen its strategic isolation following the 1989 Tiananmen Square massacre and to counter Taiwan's heightened international profile. In February 1992, China and the four former-Soviet border states – Kazakstan, Kyrgyzstan, Russia and Tajikistan – held the seventh round of demilitarisation negotiations;

so-called 'four-plus-one' talks have since been held regularly. Confidence-building-measure (CBM) and demilitarisation agreements – direct products of Yeltsin's decision to affirm Gorbachev's normalisation agenda – were reached by the presidents of the five states in April 1996 and April 1997 respectively.

Partnership

China and Russia have presented the 1996–97 agreements as developments of great strategic importance – rather than simply a further stage in the normalisation process. Vladimir Lukin, Chairman of the Russian Duma's International Affairs Committee, called the CBM agreement 'Russia's most important victory in the diplomatic field in years'.[6] Yevgeny Afanasiev, Director of the Russian Foreign Ministry's First Asia Department, went further, claiming that the 1996–97 deals 'could serve as a model for ensuring peace, security, and stability in ... Eurasia on a new, partnership footing'.[7]

Russian Objectives and Interests

Originally developed as part of its pro-Western strategy, post-Soviet Russia's first 'strategic partnership' was with the US. According to Russian analyst Sergei Kortunov, partnership was a form of interaction 'making it possible to coordinate, reconcile and formulate a common policy in respect to third countries ... [including] arms control, the nonproliferation of weapons of mass destruction and the prevention of nuclear war'.[8] Partnership involved a political and strategic commitment to secure a place in the post-Cold War world through cooperative and equal relations with the West. In February 1992, Yeltsin wrote to Japanese Prime Minister Kiichi Miyazawa, suggesting that Japan was 'a potential alliance partner'.[9] Relations with China were left to follow the normalisation course set by Gorbachev.

Within months of Yeltsin's overture to Japan, however, his strategic-partnership policy towards the West came under attack. Russian conservatives criticised Yeltsin's support for US positions on arms control and its policies towards former regions of Soviet influence such as Eastern Europe and the Middle East. At the same time, the US opposed arms sales to India and Iran that were critical to Russia's ailing defence industry and overrode Moscow's declared interests in Bosnia-Herzegovina and Iraq. Yeltsin's conflict with the communist-dominated parliament further undermined the basis of Russia's Western-oriented foreign policy and its preference for partnerships solely with the 'developed' countries of the north.[10] Russia's domestic economic and political weakness also hampered its ability to pursue a coherent international agenda. Throughout 1992 and 1993, Moscow faced the threat of Siberian secession and tensions with the Russian Far East.

Advocates of a more nationalist *realpolitik* led the assault on Yeltsin's pro-Western policy. These critics advanced a view of international political and economic relations in which Western, particularly US, interests opposed Russia's rejuvenation. They argued that the concessions made by Foreign Minister Andrei Kozyrev and by Yeltsin were strategically misconceived.[11] In the critics' view, an effective Russian foreign policy demanded a clear conception of the country's interests, a return to balance-of-power precepts and resistance to Western pressure for further economic and strategic concessions. According to this argument, Russia's southern periphery and its geographic position as a bridge between the West and the mainland Asian powers of China and India meant that it could never be exclusively Western. Its location provided an opportunity to become 'a focal point of a new Eurasian security complex'.[12] Realising Russia's great-power potential in the post-Cold War world, therefore, required the country to maintain a sphere of influence over the newly independent states of the former Soviet Union and to cultivate partnerships with China, India and Iran.

Yeltsin's decision, under pressure from nationalist opponents, to cancel at short notice a visit to Japan scheduled for September 1992 underlined the difficulties confronting his overtly pro-Western policy. By late 1992, Kozyrev and Yeltsin were forced to reorient Russia's relations with the major powers. During a visit to South Korea in November 1992, Yeltsin declared that 'nowadays our policy is being transferred from the Western European and American lines to the Asia-Pacific region and my visit here is the first move in this process'.[13] A month later, the implications of this shift became clear as Kozyrev warned a Western audience that 'partnership does not mean the rejection of a strong sometimes aggressive policy of defending one's own national interests'.[14] During his first state visit to Beijing, which took place in the same month, Yeltsin announced that 'developing Russian–Chinese relations has priority in Russia's foreign relations'.[15]

In January 1994, Yeltsin formalised this shift away from the West by elevating China to partner status. In a letter to Jiang Zemin, Secretary-General of the Communist Party of China (CPC), Yeltsin proposed that the two countries establish a 'constructive partnership geared to the needs of the twenty-first century'.[16] The letter, delivered to Jiang by Kozyrev, was followed by visits from Prime Minister Viktor Chernomyrdin, General Mikhail Kolesnikov, the Chief of the Army General Staff, and the Leader of the Duma, Ivan Rybkin. Kozyrev himself defined the proposed 'constructive partnership' as involving mutual confidence, cooperation in the United Nations Security Council (UNSC) and major growth in trade and economic cooperation.[17]

Chinese Objectives and Interests

Groups within the Chinese and Soviet leaderships had explored the possibility of closer ties following the Tiananmen Square massacre. However, Beijing's approach was based on the Five Principles of Peaceful Co-existence first outlined in the 1950s. These principles placed state sovereignty, non-interference in other countries' affairs and insistence on China's historic borders at the heart of its foreign policy. China re-affirmed this position as relations with the US cooled in the early 1980s. Alliances and power blocs were declared 'anathema' at the CPC's Twelfth Party Congress in September 1982.

China hedged its bets with Russia

When relations with the Soviet Union began to warm, Beijing sought normalisation, but shied away from any suggestion of reviving the Sino-Soviet alliance of the 1950s. As Jiang explained when he visited Moscow in May 1991, China would not 'enter into alliance or establish strategic relations with any big powers'.[18] Beijing rebuffed Yeltsin's overtures in December 1992, refusing to follow South Korea in upgrading to treaty status a Joint Statement effectively pledging non-aggression.[19] The result in the early 1990s was an arms-length, 'good-neighbour' relationship negotiated more on Chinese than Russian terms. At the same time, China hedged its strategic bets by cultivating ties with Ukraine and the Baltic states.[20]

Yeltsin's January 1994 partnership proposal was therefore a challenge to Beijing's long-standing position. In April 1994, in a belated response to Yeltsin's offer, Deng reportedly announced to the CPC Standing Committee Politburo that it was 'not advisable to be impatient to establish partnership or treaty relations' with Russia. Deng suggested that such a move was unnecessary: 'I think for quite a long time to come there will not be major conflicts between China and Russia'.[21]

Despite this rebuff, Russia's overtures coincided with intense concern in Beijing over threats to China's security. The dissident movement had been crushed in 1989, but China faced challenges from ethnic activists in Tibet, Xinjiang and Inner Mongolia, while Taiwan was becoming increasingly assertive. US and European arms embargoes instituted in the wake of the Tiananmen Square massacre undermined China's ability to confront these difficulties, while the victory of the US-led coalition over Iraq in the Gulf crisis of 1990–91 underscored Beijing's limited military capabilities and heightened Chinese fears about US global intentions. China saw a multipolar post-Cold War world as most likely to foster its political and economic development. Perceived US 'hegemony' became a threat to this new order, and to Beijing's preference for rigid principles of state sovereignty.[22] Russia's appeals to partnership therefore chimed with China's concerns about the implications of US strength.

These concerns grew against a background of increasing nationalist sentiment within the Chinese political and military leadership and a growing desire to adopt a more forceful stance against Washington. In September 1992, Foreign Minister Qian Qichen argued in an internal Party speech that:

> *the USA's hegemonic stance and its attempts to interfere in the internal affairs of other states pose the greatest danger to socialist China. To weaken pressure from Washington, China must broaden relations with Japan, Russia, South Korea and other neighbouring countries.*[23]

In April and September 1993, Admiral Liu Huaqing, architect of the Chinese military's modernisation programme, and Defence Minister Chi Haotian reportedly presented petitions from senior military officers demanding a more 'principled' approach to trade disputes with the US.[24] Deng apparently opposed an anti-US coalition, but recognised the increasing importance of a relationship with Russia in counter-balancing Washington.[25] In 1993, two secret documents were reported to have been relayed to Politburo members and CPC and military officials suggesting that a recast relationship with Russia would be 'a new strategic move to prevent US hegemonism from subverting China and intervening in the internal affairs of other Asian countries'.[26] In mid-1994, the Hong Kong press reported that senior sections of the CPC supported good-neighbour relations with Russia – 'in contrast to Deng's unique view' – as a counter to the US and as a means to circumvent Tiananmen-inspired sanctions on arms and high-technology sales.[27]

Important Soviet alumni within the Chinese leadership bolstered Russia's appeal as a diplomatic and economic counter-weight to the US, particularly when Deng's involvement in decision-making declined. Jiang was trained at Moscow's Stalin Autoworks, a show-case of Soviet industry, in the 1950s, and was persecuted during the Cultural Revolution for his Soviet connections. Liu, a prominent advocate of increased purchases of Russian weaponry, was trained at the Voroshilov Naval Academy in Leningrad. These links strengthened the stature of Chinese leaders such as Jiang and Prime Minister Li Peng, a graduate of the Moscow Power Institute, as international statesmen and consolidated their power bases in preparation for the post-Deng succession.

In late May 1994, Jiang informed Chernomyrdin that China was 'willing to join Russia in raising Sino-Russian relations to a new level', and set the date for his first visit to Russia since the collapse of the Soviet Union.[28] During their first presidential summit in September 1994, Yeltsin and Jiang issued a Joint Statement outlining a constructive partnership and claiming their determination 'as they look toward the twenty-first century, to raise relations between the two countries to a qualitatively new level, thereby opening up to the full and making use of the considerable potential of Russian–Chinese cooperation'.[29]

From 'Constructive' to 'Strategic' Partners

The 1994 Jiang–Yeltsin summit signalled a limited consensus within the two countries on the value of elevating bilateral relations to a new level. In Russia, support for closer links spanned nationalist, communist and centrist political groupings. Nevertheless, it remained coupled with a deep suspicion of China's long-term intentions, an awareness of Russia's declining economic and strategic position, and the continued importance of relations with the US. Anxiety and outright opposition to stronger ties with China were regularly expressed. A loose grouping of like-minded individuals, rather than a coherent – let alone realistic – articulation of national interests bound together supporters of closer relations.[30]

China's commitment was pragmatic and limited. Beijing had little faith in Russia's economic prospects and was wary of the implications of closer links for its independent foreign policy.[31] As a result, China resisted Russian attempts to enhance the relationship with rhetorical gloss. It insisted on the September 1994 formulation that the constructive partnership 'did not have the nature of an alliance and [is] not directed against any third country', but merely outlined broad parameters of coordination on bilateral and international issues.[32] Despite intensive talks over the meaning of the constructive partnership, the bulk of bilateral relations remained devoted to resolving outstanding normalisation issues.

Elements within Russia, however, continued to press for a more expansive relationship. As early as January 1994, Kozyrev spoke of 'strategic' rather than simply 'constructive' partnership. Jiang told Chernomyrdin in May 1994 that China looked to relations with Russia from a 'strategic point of view'.[33] However, when Defence Minister Pavel Grachev suggested that Russia and China should 'solve the problems of security together', Beijing reiterated that it 'would not create such an alliance', preferring instead to be 'good neighbours, good partners and good friends'.[34]

Yeltsin and Jiang's fourth presidential summit, originally scheduled for late 1995, was expected to be part of that process, providing a venue for signing the five-nation CBM agreement. However, by the time the summit took place in April 1996, the atmosphere between Russia and China had changed: just 24 hours before the meeting, Yeltsin telephoned Jiang from his stop-over in Khabarovsk, formally proposing that the two establish a 'strategic partnership for the twenty-first century'. Jiang immediately accepted the proposal. The key elements of this partnership were:

- deeper political and economic ties;
- increased two-way trade (to $20bn by 2000);
- multilateral security arrangements, possibly serving as a model in the Asia-Pacific region;
- coordinated positions on the UNSC;
- respect for national sovereignty and non-interference in each other's domestic affairs; and
- a commitment to a multipolar world order.

China's sudden decision formally to adopt a strategic partnership was prompted by heightened concern over US power and Moscow's determination to place its relationship with Beijing on the same footing as that with Washington. By early 1996, what support remained in Russia for stronger relations with the West had been undermined by NATO's decision in December 1994 to consider including former Warsaw Pact states, and the weakening and eventual dismissal of Foreign Minister Kozyrev in favour of Yevgeni Primakov.[35] As former head of the Foreign Intelligence Service, Primakov had been a central figure in galvanising early opposition to NATO enlargement.[36] From his appointment in January 1996, Primakov explicitly advocated balancing US power through relations with China and developing parallel strategic partnerships with India and Iran. Under Primakov, the Russian Foreign Ministry officially claimed the priority status of the relationship with Beijing; Chernomyrdin promoted the interests of the industrial, energy and arms sectors trading with China. Opponents of the relationship at the core of the Yeltsin government were identified by their failure to support it, rather than by their active opposition. For example, by late 1997, First Deputy Prime Minister Anatoli Chubais, one of the most liberal members of the inner circle, was the only senior figure not to have visited China.[37] Defence Minister Igor Rodionov's December 1996 suggestion that China was enlarging its influence at Russia's expense and might be a future threat was followed by a series of denials and public statements supporting the relationship.[38] China became part of a Russian policy of 'equal partnership' with all major powers. Russian analysts supportive of official overtures began to speak of a relationship with Beijing that satisfied many of Moscow's economic and strategic concerns.[39] Links with China would improve Russia's trade balance, open markets for high-technology exports and provide leverage against the US in Asia, Europe and international organisations.[40]

At the same time, Beijing's relations with Taipei, Washington and Tokyo weakened in the run-up to the first Taiwanese presidential elections, culminating in a stand-off in the Taiwan Strait in March 1996. Relations were also strained by the reaffirmation of the US–Japan Security Treaty the following month. Pessimistic assessments of the prospects for improved Sino-US ties were reported within Beijing. According to one Hong Kong newspaper, a study by the Chinese Central Policy Research Centre, approved in March 1996 by the State Council, concluded that it was 'impossible for China and the United States to establish a friendly and cooperative partnership' and that a 'limited' war with the US was possible.[41] Chinese

China sees long-term rivalry with the US

analysts saw similar difficulties facing US–Russia ties. Although short-term cooperation with the US was essential to Russian development, analysts suggested that Washington was pursuing a hegemonic strategy that required the long-term containment of Russian interests.[42] Furthermore, China feared for its own stability should Russian internal control weaken further. Foreign Ministry reports in January 1995 and May 1996 apparently emphasised the benefits to China of a Yeltsin victory in presidential elections in 1996. One such report warned:

> *Changes in Russia will have the greatest influence on Northwestern China ... We should closely follow the situation in Russia and its relations with our northern borders. Unlike some Western countries, we do not want chaos in Russia.*[43]

Rhetoric or Substance?
Russia and China have found more common ground on relations with the US than either could have anticipated as the Cold War ended. Elite political links have consequently warmed, particularly since 1995. Nevertheless, China and Russia hold fundamentally different views of what strategic partnership involves. For Russia,

the relationship has deep – albeit contentious – political and philo-sophical roots. Yeltsin insists that the partnership has 'enormous, and perhaps even historic, significance, inasmuch as we are determining the fate of the 21st century'.[44] China's leaders have been far more cautious, repeatedly playing down elements of the relationship and placing it in the context of longer-standing traditions of adherence to the Five Principles of Peaceful Co-existence and aversion to bloc or alliance politics. Jiang's agreement to upgrade links from 'constructive' to 'strategic' partnership on 24-hours' notice, rather than seeking agreement from other Chinese leaders, appears to confirm that no significant departure from China's foreign-policy stance of independence and pragmatism has taken place. China's interest in improved bilateral ties remains the completion of the original normalisation negotiations concerning border demarcation and open economic links. Although Jiang has agreed to describe relations as a 'strategic partnership', China has often backed away from Russian definitions of what this actually means. China's preferred formulation of the phrase – managing bilateral relations 'strategically with an eye on the twenty-first century' – is the same as that used *vis-à-vis* its relations with Japan.[45] Jiang described links with the US as a 'strategic partnership' after a trip there in October 1997.

Is Sino-Russian strategic partnership simply a cliché glossing over the difficulties faced by two major powers with unstable pasts? Or are Russia and China developing, as they both insist, a long-term relationship similar to that sought by many US policy-makers with China: 'a common strategic framework to deepen areas of common interest and manage disagreements'?[46] The domestic and inter-national concerns that Russia and China share in the late 1990s imply that partnership is, as both countries repeatedly stress, a logical and incremental development from normalisation. The following three chapters address these questions in depth.

chapter 2

Bilateral Relations

The Sino-Russian strategic partnership is premised on establishing a stable bilateral relationship. This necessitates developing political, economic and personal ties to entrench and expand relations and to complete border and demilitarisation negotiations. Since 1992, these objectives of normalisation and partnership have been pursued simultaneously, but unevenly.

An unprecedented number of ministerial, parliamentary, military and media visits and exchanges has taken place since the early 1990s. Official contacts have been established between the Chinese and Russian Communist Parties, and – more significantly – with Prime Minister Chernomyrdin's 'Our Home is Russia' parliamentary faction and between the Russian and Chinese parliaments.[1] According to the Russian Ambassador to China, 'there exist no political barriers' to growing bilateral relations.[2] Beginning in April 1996, Jiang and Yeltsin agreed to meet at least annually; a 'hot line' between the two has reportedly since been established.[3] In December 1996, a six-monthly Prime Ministerial Commission was established to initial bilateral trade and cooperation agreements.

However, key Russian sectors have strongly opposed closer ties with China. In the face of volatile bilateral trade and contentious border and demilitarisation agreements, Yeltsin's government has been forced to operate within a restricted mandate, effectively giving priority to an élite political relationship over the pragmatic approach originally envisaged by Deng and Gorbachev.

Politics and Society

In the early 1990s, there was little basis for a strong and open bilateral relationship between China and Russia. During the late nineteenth and early twentieth centuries, ethnic Russians co-existed with Manchurians, Chinese, Koreans and Japanese on both sides of the border. However, Soviet policy enforced ethnic exclusion to strengthen its control over the Far East, and the last remnants of the Chinese presence in the region disappeared in the 1960s. Until 1983, only one border crossing existed and, even when Sino-Soviet relations began to improve in the 1980s, contacts were tightly controlled. Only 10,000 Chinese workers were permitted to enter Primorskii Krai, Russia's so-called 'gateway to the Pacific', and, until 1986, postal links and telephone connections were either non-existent or available only through Moscow and Beijing.[4]

The collapse of the Soviet Union sharply increased cross-border contacts. During his visit to Beijing in 1992, Yeltsin agreed to lift many of the visa restrictions impeding cross-border trade. A year later, 13 ports, four bridges and three airports spanned the longest section of the border, between Heilongjiang and the Russian Far East; the Chinese State Council had authorised three border cities – Heihe, Suifenhe and Hunchun – to pursue cross-border trade; and China had opened a consulate in Vladivostok.[5] Bilateral trade grew significantly, primarily the result of efforts by small-scale, 'suitcase' merchants selling low-quality consumer goods.[6] Some 751,000 Chinese citizens reportedly visited Russia during 1993, 200,000 of whom are believed to have crossed at one checkpoint alone. An estimated 777,000 Russians travelled the other way.[7]

Far Eastern Regional Politics

Closer links with China rapidly became a sensitive issue in Russian regional politics. Since 1992–93, cross-border ties have been influenced by a conservative realignment in the Russian Far East that has undermined support for more open borders.

During the transition from Soviet to Russian rule, the Far East was dominated by a group of liberal and reformist administrators who actively sought foreign investment and, initially, appeared willing to put aside nationalist political platforms. However, following the collapse of Yeltsin's Japan initiative in 1992, regional politics took a nationalist and populist turn. From May 1993, a

Map 2 *The Russian Far East and northern China*

succession of Soviet-style managerial and industrial *nomenklatura* took power in the Far East: Yevgeni Krasnoyarov (Sakhalinskaya Oblast); Yevgeni Nazdratenko (Primorskii Krai); Vladimir Polevanov (Amurskaya Oblast); and Viktor Ishaev (Khabarovskii Krai). These leaders sought to enhance or reinstate Soviet-era economic privileges and subsidies for their impoverished regions. All were eager to gain greater leverage over Moscow; several were corrupt and authoritarian.[8]

Primorskii Krai under Nazdratenko has been the most notorious example. Although aligned with industrial interests in Chernomyrdin's circle, Nazdratenko opposed Yeltsin's economic and foreign policies and flirted with separatist sentiment in the Far East. He also threatened the balance of power between the region and Moscow, in a bid to undermine the Yeltsin government's ability to make policy on the Far East's behalf, by attempting to gain control of the Kuril Islands/Northern Territories at the expense of neighbouring Sakhalinskaya Oblast. At the same time, he cracked down on opposition in Primorskii Krai.

Russian regional resistance to détente

Nazdratenko seized on concerns over the apparently growing Chinese presence to challenge Sino-Russian border demarcation. Throughout 1992 and 1993, the Russian press reported running totals of Chinese reputed to be in the region. Between 200,000 and two million illegal Chinese immigrants were estimated to be in the Russian Federation in 1993–94.[9] Nazdratenko's administration claimed that 150,000 Chinese 'overstayers' were present in Primorskii Krai alone. Chinese traders were blamed for rising crime rates in border cities and accused of profiteering from privatisations, creating housing shortages and fuelling unemployment rates.[10] In Vladivostok, one analyst suggested that a Chinese autonomous province would be established in the region within 30 years.[11]

These fears were greatly exaggerated. *Operation Foreigner*, the Russian Border Guard's attempt to clamp down on illegal immigration from China, netted its largest single haul in November 1996, when just 22 illegal immigrants were caught trying to enter Primorskii Krai.[12] According to one Russian analyst, only 87 Chinese have settled permanently in Amurskaya Oblast since 1987, and 170 in Khabarovskii Krai.[13] Nevertheless, the perceived 'immigration crisis' provided an opportunity for Far Eastern governors to assert their views on Russia's appropriate relationship with China.

Since 1994, Nazdratenko has led regional opposition to the 1991 border-demarcation agreement. In February 1995, just before Kozyrev was to start an official visit to China, Nazdratenko called for sections of the agreement ceding parts of the border region to China to be revised, declaring 'as long as I am governor I will not give up even a metre of soil'.[14] He has threatened to resign should territory be handed over, claiming that it contained the graves of Russian soldiers, along with prime hunting and agricultural land. Russian concessions would also, it was claimed, restore Chinese access to the Sea of Japan.[15] In Khabarovskii Krai, foreigners wishing to stay for more than three days were required to register with the local authorities, while Primorskii Krai banned Chinese citizens from owning or leasing property, and imposed a daily residence tax. As a result, in 1993 the federal government was forced to renegotiate the visa-free-travel regime with China. Implementation of the new regime coincided with the Chinese New Year, reportedly barring thousands of Chinese who had returned home for the holiday from re-entering Russia.[16] Potential 'overstayers' were further deterred by requirements that they purchase visas from the Russian consulate in advance, and that they pay in US dollars.[17]

Nazdratenko and his fellow Far Eastern governors have also opposed joint infrastructure development and accused China of seeking to exploit Russian resources through 'economic colonisation'. The Russian Far Eastern media cited Chinese rail and road links ending at the border as evidence of China's long-term territorial ambitions. Local Russian administrations stalled transport projects. Amurskaya Oblast, although the worst hit of all Russian border areas by the post-Soviet downturn in trade, refused until 1996 to match Chinese offers to fund half the construction costs of a bridge across the Amur River. Although China was the largest investor in the region in 1993, local officials polled on their preferred investment partners listed it a distant fourth (with 4%) after the US (64%), Japan (44%) and South Korea (16%).[18]

The most obvious victim of these tensions is the Tumen River Project promoted by China's Jilin province under the auspices of the United Nations Development Programme (UNDP). Launched in 1991, the project sought to bring China, Mongolia, North and South

Korea and Russia together to develop a trade and development zone at the mouth of the Tumen River Delta. China, along with the two Koreas and Mongolia, pushed the project forward; politicians in the Russian Far East, however, vigorously opposed it. China was accused of seeking to use the project to gain access to the Sea of Japan, thereby bypassing Russian transport and processing facilities and enabling further illegal immigration.[19] As one local academic explained: 'It is highly improbable that the consortium members will lavish charity on Russia; they are far more likely to be frugal in their spending and to confine themselves to ... Chinese territory'.[20]

Yeltsin's Limited China 'Mandate'

Nazdratenko, whom Yeltsin threatened with dismissal in early 1996, has been able to challenge Moscow's conduct of relations with China because of Yeltsin's limited mandate to deepen the partnership. Despite widespread agreement in Moscow that Beijing should be a political 'partner', there is no common understanding of what this would mean for Russia. There is deep disagreement about the merits of pursuing closer ties and the long-term consequences of exporting Russian civilian and defence high technology to an irredentist and possibly unstable emerging power.[21] Even those who support the agreements reached to date, such as International Affairs Committee Chairman Lukin, fear that 'the alignment of power between Russia and China has changed drastically and not in our favour'.[22]

These debates reflect the fact that Moscow cannot maintain its past levels of control over Russia's Far East, and that its position is declining as China's strength grows. As former Prime Minister Yegor Gaidar explained in 1995: 'With our weakness, our huge unassimilated territories in the Far East, we provoke a threat'.[23] As in European Russia, the Far East's population has fallen from a peak in 1991 of 8.1m to 7.8m.[24] By contrast, some 74m people live in Heilongjiang and Jilin, and over 100m in the north-east as a whole (Heilongjiang, Jilin, Liaoning and Inner Mongolia). Former Deputy Prime Minister Sergei Shakrai has claimed that the population could decline by as much as two-thirds by 2010, warning that 'for the first time in four centuries China has surpassed Russia's rate of economic growth'.

Alongside the recognition that China poses a long-term demographic, economic and strategic challenge to Russia lie the considerable benefits to key industrial groups close to the Yeltsin government of an open cross-border relationship and high-technology transfers. Despite talk of a long-term relationship, 'in the short run China's most important effect on Russia is as a market, trading partner and purchaser of arms'.[25] During a Yeltsin–Jiang summit in April 1997, the liberal newspaper *Segodnya* bemoaned: 'all these curtseys toward each other, as well as verbal criticism of the West, tend to resemble propagandistic, rather than political cooperation'.[26]

Trade and Economics

The Yeltsin government's shift to élite-led relations with China has been mirrored by a structural change in the nature of Sino-Russian trade. In April 1996, Russia and China announced their $20bn two-way trade target by 2000, twice the goal agreed a year earlier. Russian officials point to agreements signed since 1996 as evidence of efforts to increase growth, and trade has indeed risen from $5.5bn in 1995 to $6.9bn in 1996, with an optimistic $8bn forecast for 1997.

These figures conceal a 'boom and bust' cycle that is primitive and unsustainable. Before 1994, renewed Sino-Russian trade appeared set to contribute to a long-term improvement in bilateral relations. The removal of visa restrictions and reopened border crossings were accompanied by efforts in both China and Russia to liberalise trade. In 1992, Vladivostok declared itself an open city and announced a 'Greater Vladivostok Project', with plans to modernise port facilities and develop international transport infrastructure.[27] Further along the coast, the port city of Nakhodka launched the region's only free economic zone (FEZ), securing European Bank for Reconstruction and Development (EBRD) feasibility-study funding and pledges of tax relief from Moscow. Chinese construction workers and contract labourers travelled to the region, and 90 registered Chinese joint ventures were set up in the Nakhodka FEZ. Some 61% of new joint ventures in Vladivostok were with the Chinese. A consumer-goods shortage in the Far East in 1991–92, and decisions by local authorities and enterprises to sell off stocks – such as trucks and fertilisers – at a substantially discounted price, further boosted trade.

Trade growth reached record highs between 1991 and 1993. By 1993, China was Russia's second-largest trading partner – official commerce alone accounted for 35% of Russia's total business with

Table I *Russian Far East Trade with China, 1995–1996*

(US$m, %)	1995			1996		
	Export	Import	Total	Export	Import	Total
Total	166.2	153.9	320.1	743.5	199.8	943.3
	100.0	*100.0*	*100.0*	*100.0*	*100.0*	*100.0*
Khabarovskii Krai						
	32.7	45.9	78.6	501.0	49.2	550.2
	19.7	*29.8*	*24.6*	*67.4*	*24.6*	*58.2*
Primorskii Krai						
	43.7	67.1	110.8	110.0	90.7	200.7
	26.3	*43.6*	*34.6*	*14.8*	*45.4*	*21.3*
Amurskaya Oblast						
	32.4	22.1	54.5	35.4	29.4	64.8
	19.5	*14.4*	*17.0*	*4.8*	*14.7*	*6.9*
Kamchatskaya Oblast						
	51.1	9.1	60.2	46.1	18.6	64.7
	30.7	*5.9*	*18.8*	*6.2*	*9.3*	*6.9*
Sakhalinskaya Oblast						
	5.0	4.0	9.0	50.0	10.0	60.0
	3.0	*2.6*	*2.8*	*6.7*	*5.0*	*6.4*
Republic of Sakha (Yakutia)						
	0.7	5.3	6.0	0.3	1.5	1.8
	0.4	*3.4*	*1.9*	*0.04*	*0.8*	*0.2*
Magadanskaya Oblast						
	0.6	0.4	1.0	0.7	0.4	1.1
	0.4	*0.3*	*0.3*	*0.1*	*0.2*	*0.1*

Source Japan External Trade Organisation, *Eastern Europe Newsletter*, August 1997

Asia – while Russia was China's seventh.[28] Border trade between the Far East and neighbouring Chinese provinces constituted up to 80% of Russia's total trade with China.[29] Heilongjiang recorded over $2bn-worth of exports to Russia in 1993; Khabarovsk sourced two-thirds of its imports from China. Nearly half of Khabarovsk's foreign trade was conducted with China in 1993 (43.5%, or $302.5m).[30] Primorskii Krai and Amurskaya Oblast registered similar levels of exports.

Commentators began to speculate that regional trade was set to overtake government-to-government contacts as the driving force of closer bilateral ties. It was not to be. The 1991–92 economic crisis in the Far East undermined the basis of the crucial barter-trade system. Russians were largely unable to repay Chinese exporters.[31] Dubious business practices and poor-quality goods were widely reported on both sides. Inadequate transport infrastructure and high tariffs hampered Russian exporters. According to Russian officials, limited transport blocked 25–30% of deals.[32] As a result, Russian exports were neither profitable nor reliable. These problems were compounded by the visa-regime renegotiation of 1993 and Moscow's subsequent decisions to impose steep import and export duties, cut transport subsidies and place restrictions on organisations entitled to engage in foreign trade. Those licensed to trade were subject to quotas and required to surrender half their hard-currency earnings in exchange for roubles and compulsory state-purchase orders.[33] Moscow then failed to implement comprehensive foreign-investment legislation or adequate banking facilities to stabilise the situation.

As a result, two-way trade dropped from its 1993 high of $7.7bn to $5bn the following year and $5.5bn in 1995. Primorkskii

Table 2 *Chinese Trade with the Soviet Union/Russia, 1986–1996*

(US$m)	Exports	Imports	Total two-way trade	Balance
1986*	1,230	1,472	2,702	-242
1987*	1,247	1,291	2,538	-44
1988*	1,476	1,802	3,278	-326
1989*	1,849	2,147	3,996	-298
1990*	2,048	2,213	4,261	-99
1991*	1,823	2,081	3,904	-258
1992	2,337	3,512	5,849	-1,175
1993	2,692	4,986	7,678	-2,294
1994	1,578	3,466	5,044	-1,888
1995	1,674	3,799	5,473	-2,125
1996	1,693	5,156	6,849	-3,463

Note *trade with the Soviet Union
Source IMF, *Direction of Trade Statistics Yearbook*, various years

Krai's trade with China fell by 78%. In Amurskaya Oblast, border commerce collapsed by 81% between the first quarters of 1993 and 1994 (from $100m to $19m).[34] The decline continued in 1995.[35] Heilongjiang saw trade drop by 45% between the first quarter of 1993 and that of 1994. New joint ventures registered in Russia fell from a peak of 56 in 1993 to only four in the first five months of 1995.[36] Despite presidential commitments to raise trade to new heights, the two countries are still struggling to regain the levels of 1993.

Managed Trade, Divergent Interests

Russia's initial partnership proposals coincided with the onset of this trade crisis. As the extent of the slump – and of the anti-Chinese campaign by Russian Far Eastern politicians – became clear, high-level Moscow officials were dispatched to Beijing to reassure the Chinese that immigration and border-trade tensions would not undermine wider progress in bilateral relations. In accepting the 1994 constructive-partnership proposal during the September Moscow summit, Jiang addressed the trade crisis at length. He explained that, as long as the overall goal of developing stable relations was borne in mind, 'these problems accompanying our advancement and development are not difficult to solve'.[37] Russian studies were cited to the effect that payment problems and limited transport infrastructure were the greatest hurdles to the smooth expansion of trade.[38] As a result, a series of Sino-Russian government talks focused on developing better-regulated ties, with both Yeltsin and Jiang emphasising the need to confine border trade to 'normal' levels.

However, China and Russia differ over the means to improve trading links. Beijing recognises the tensions generated by unregulated, poor-quality trade, and has moved to restrict some of its elements. But China is also wary of Russia's unstable investment climate. Despite calls for greater government support for Chinese businesses operating in Russia and the Commonwealth of Independent States (CIS), China's goal remains to develop its land-locked north-eastern provinces. Inner Mongolia, Heilongjiang and Jilin all rely on trade

differences over how to improve trade relations

with Russia for economic development. As a result, Chinese central and regional authorities have focused on insulating border trade from further slumps and building infrastructure. Free-trade zones are planned on the border at Zabaykalsk and Manzhouli and in Heihe (Heilongjiang province).[39]

By 1996, these efforts had met with some success. In October, China reported the completion of its 81km section of railway which will eventually link Jilin with Zarubino; a long-delayed bridge project with Amurskaya Oblast was approved; and, in 1997, a fibre-optic cable link was established between Harbin and Khabarovsk.[40] As a result, border trade picked up significantly for the first time since 1993, aided by Chinese tariff exemptions and quality checks.[41] Moscow curbed Far Eastern opposition to greater trade with China. Primakov expressed his impatience with opposition to the Tumen River Project and, in June 1997, a memorandum establishing a Russian-Chinese Committee on Regional Border Trade and Economic Cooperation was signed during the second session of the Prime Ministerial Commission.[42]

Despite these moves, the Yeltsin government's general trade strategy towards China has shifted since 1993 from encouraging cross-border links to a more managed, centralised relationship focusing on key industries such as energy, nuclear power, heavy machinery and defence. Russian companies tendered to build heavy machinery for the Three Gorges Dam hydroelectric scheme on the Yangtze River. They also undertook to build a nuclear-power plant in Jiangsu province and a uranium-enrichment plant in Shanxi. The Yeltsin government promoted both projects as examples of the benefits of strategic partnership, claiming that they will create thousands of Russian jobs and significantly increase two-way trade. Russia and China have announced a joint venture to explore gas reserves in Irkutskaya Oblast and to build a gas pipeline to South Korea via Mongolia and China. A framework agreement governing the pipeline project – expected to cost $12bn – was signed in November 1997.[43] Gazprom announced in 1996 that it would sign a contract with the Chinese Oil and Gas Corporation to develop fields in China.[44] A high-voltage power line is also planned from Eastern Siberia to China. Russian aerospace industries are keenly interested in Chinese markets. Aviastar, Russia's largest commercial-aircraft manufacturer, is attempting to sell short-haul airliners; plans have been mooted for a joint Sino-Russian airline and for Russian aircraft-maintenance facilities in China.[45] Russia has also undertaken to build a spacecraft in China and to cooperate in launching a rocket capable of carrying a 20-tonne spaceship into orbit.[46]

Defence sales have been the highest-profile element of Russia's trade strategy. With the exception of a brief lull in 1993, Russia's share of the Chinese arms market has grown steadily, making it China's largest source of overseas arms by far. Between 1990 and 1995, the Soviet Union/Russia sold weapons worth between $2.9bn and $6.0bn.[47] In 1996, Russian exports to China reportedly exceeded $2.1bn, amounting to nearly 70% of China's total arms imports.[48]

Russian officials have harnessed the strategic partnership in a bid to facilitate these deals. Foreign Ministry officials have repeatedly spoken of the 'real content' needed if partnership is to be meaningful, warning that the level of economic activity has been 'embarrassingly small'.[49] The results of the constructive partnership had to be made 'manifest' – 'real partnership is impossible without economic integration'.[50] The bureaucratic framework of the partnership has been designed to advance Moscow's preferred trade agenda. The twice-yearly Prime Ministerial Committee and its numerous preparatory sub-committees are intended to promote bilateral deals.

Using diplomatic ties to encourage trade is not new, but Russia's approach is particularly heavy-handed. In addition, many deals cited as evidence of the strategic partnership are covered only by framework agreements or protocols of intent, or are in the earliest planning stages. Despite Russia's expectations, China is unwilling to provide it with preferential access to high-profile projects. Russian officials were dismayed by the country's failure in September 1997 to win any of the $800m-worth of tenders for the Three Gorges Dam project. Chinese agreement to move ahead with the Jiangsu nuclear-power plant has also proved elusive. China's apparent wish to restart nuclear-technology cooperation with the US, embargoed since the late 1980s, and to regain access to French defence exports highlights the stiff competition Russia faces. Without a greater share of the Russian market, China has little interest in boosting Russia's export trade.

Nevertheless, the Yeltsin government is likely to persist with the élite-driven relationship because it is profitable and because Moscow fears the consequences of open borders. Russia enjoys a substantial trade surplus with China and a net tax surplus with the regions of the Far East. In 1996, Russia had a $3.5bn trade surplus

Russia will persist with the élite-driven relationship

with China. Primorskii and Khabarovskii Krais pay 39% and 38% respectively of their tax revenues directly to Moscow. Expanded regional trade would redress the imbalance between Russia and China to China's benefit and force Moscow to renegotiate its fiscal relationships with the Far East.

In the short term, Moscow has tended to view the strategic partnership, with its limited cross-border trade and emphasis on government-to-government deals, as preserving the status quo and hence its control over a situation in which it appears to hold the weakest hand. Yeltsin's preferred 'normal and natural' level of trade limits Chinese commercial challenges in the Far East and allows regional politicians to stall joint projects. The impoverished and unequal fiscal arrangements between Moscow and the governments of the Russian Far East constrain regional opposition to central government. This strategy has, however, had a destabilising effect in that the region's only means of registering its concerns in Moscow is to play to the centre's fears of losing strategic control to China, while China itself has no real economic stake in the relationship. As analyst Stephen Blank explains:

> The deliberate neglect of Asiatic Russia actually helped trigger Nazdratenko's actions, the rising xenophobia about Chinese immigration, and ultimately the problems in completing border and military agreements.[51]

In addition, Russia's belief that trade with China can grow through government fiat rather than by genuine commercial agreement has generated unrealistic expectations of the benefits of strategic partnership. By November 1997, with the Three Gorges Dam bid rejected, no agreement on the Jiangsu nuclear project and preliminary Chinese figures showing a 14.7% drop in two-way trade in the first six months of the year, Russian leaders were beginning to

Table 3 *Soviet/Russian Forces in the Russian Far East, 1989–1997*

	1989–90	1990–91	1991–92
Ground forces			
Tank divisions	3	3	3
Motor rifle divisions	21	18	18
Pacific Fleet			
Submarines	120	110	98
SSBN*	24	24	24
Principal surface combatants	77	69	63
Carriers	2	2	2
Cruisers	11	15	14
Destroyers	8	7	7
Frigates	56	45	40

*nuclear-fuelled ballistic-missile submarines

Source IISS, *The Military Balance 1997/98* (Oxford: Oxford University Press for the IISS, 1997)

criticise China, rather than their own trade strategy, for the gulf between projected and actual levels of cross-border commerce.[52]

Demilitarisation and Border Demarcation

The Yeltsin government inherited two sets of Sino-Russian border negotiations when the Soviet Union collapsed. One sought to establish a demilitarised zone along the Sino-Soviet boundary; the other to resolve outstanding border-demarcation issues.

Demilitarisation

During the Sino-Soviet split from the mid-1960s, China demanded that the Soviet Union reduce its armed forces to 1963 levels. The demand was not met, although in 1989 Gorbachev agreed in principle to demilitarisation. In June 1990, Sino-Soviet negotiators agreed to begin talks. 'Four-plus-one' demilitarisation negotiations began between China, Russia, Kazakstan, Kyrgyzstan and Tajikistan in 1992. Agreement was reached in December to withdraw troops

1992–93	1993–94	1994–95	1995–96	1996–97
3	3	3	3	0
16	16	16	13	10
86	66	51	51	43
21	20	16	18	14
54	49	50	49	45
1	0	0	0	0
13	14	9	9	4
7	7	6	6	7
33	28	35	34	34

from a 100km-wide stretch either side of the border, and to reduce offensive-weapon numbers in the zone. At the same time, Yeltsin and Jiang issued their joint declaration promising to keep troop levels to a minimum outside the zone and forswore the use of military force, effectively creating a non-aggression pact.[53] Rumours that the demilitarisation negotiations were almost complete appeared as early as September 1993.[54] However, demilitarisation talks proved more time-consuming and controversial than anticipated, concluding only in 1997.

Russian concerns over the concessions required to make demilitarisation possible slowed agreement. Russian diplomats and press reports suggested that Chinese reluctance to release precise troop-deployment levels hampered negotiations, along with China's insistence on a 300km-deep zone.[55] In truth, Russia lacked strategic depth in the Far East, and the 100km buffer posed a significant political and logistic challenge. Russia's military and strategic assets and major regional population centres all fall within the 100km zone;

China's do not. The Chinese People's Liberation Army (PLA)'s strategy of luring the enemy deep into its territory before counter-attacking meant that most military forces were deployed up to 400km from the border. Full Russian demilitarisation in the 100km zone required a withdrawal beyond the Trans-Siberian railway, perceived 'exposure' of Khabarovsk and other major Far Eastern cities, and massive redeployment of Russia's impoverished military. It also entailed implementing much-delayed military reform.

While demilitarisation talks dragged on, smaller, related deals were concluded. In May 1994, Russia and China signed an 'Agreement on the Sino-Russian Border Management System'. Two months later, agreement was reached to prevent military accidents such as unintentional border crossings and radar jamming, inadvertent missile launches and violations of airspace.[56] On 3 September 1994, a joint communiqué pledged no-first-use and non-targeting of nuclear missiles. The following May, three Chinese warships docked at Vladivostok for the first formal overseas visit by a communist Chinese naval taskforce. By the end of 1994, Russian Pacific Fleet Commander Admiral Felix Gromov had suggested the possibility of joint naval exercises. Russia invited Chinese troops to attend the *Amur-96* command-staff exercises. The Chinese extended a similar invitation in response. As Defence Minister Grachev explained after the 1994 accident-prevention agreement was signed, 'we now have more contacts, more meetings, more confidence in each other'.[57]

To break the deadlock in the main demilitarisation negotiations, the talks were split. In April 1996, China and the four ex-Soviet boundary states signed the CBM agreement, 'On Confidence Building in the Military Field in the Border Area'. The agreement confirmed the 100km demilitarisation zone, and restricted military activity within it to ensure that no side could 'attack another Party, conduct any military activity threatening to the other Party and upsetting calm and stability in the area'.[58] Provisions included an outright ban on exercises exceeding 40,000 personnel, compulsory observers for those over 35,000, and a limit of one exercise each year of 25,000 personnel or above. The arms-reduction component was finally completed in April 1997. Although not publicly available until ratified by all five nations' parliaments, the agreement reportedly stipulates that all parties must reduce their military forces to the minimum required for defence. It also limits Chinese and

Table 4 *Chinese Military Forces in Shenyang and Lanzhou Military Regions, 1996*

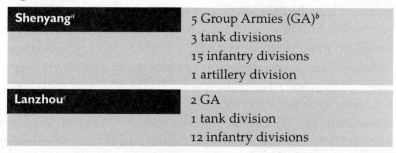

Shenyang[a]	5 Group Armies (GA)[b]
	3 tank divisions
	15 infantry divisions
	1 artillery division
Lanzhou[c]	2 GA
	1 tank division
	12 infantry divisions

Notes   [a] Shenyang Military Region = Heilongjiang, Jilin, Liaoning
  [b] GA = 60–90,000 personnel
  [c] Lanzhou Military Region includes Xinjiang, Ningxia, Shaanxi, Gansu, Qinghai

Source IISS, *The Military Balance 1997/98*

former Soviet land-force numbers, short-range aviation and anti-aircraft defences deployed within the 100km zone. Under the agreement, Russia and the three Central Asian border states must reduce troop levels by 15% within two years to a maximum of 130,400. All four states are allowed a maximum of 3,810 tanks and 4,500 armoured vehicles.[59] Chinese forces are already well below these limits, but are not expected to increase materially without external justification and consultation.

Demilitarisation agreements encapsulate hybrid messages and ambitions. Russian officials crowed over the international significance of the 1996 and 1997 deals, claiming that they represented a 'completely new security concept' and emphasised that other states could become signatories. Yeltsin claimed they were 'unprecedented for Asia and the Pacific Region'.[60] Elements within the Russian Foreign Ministry would like to see the agreements used as a basis for an Asian multilateral security framework, thereby securing

agreements merely codify reality

Russia a place in regional strategic debates. However, China has shown no such interest: the agreements simply codify 'the situation that has existed in the border region for some time'.[61] The Russian Far East military had not conducted exercises on the level restricted by the 1996 CBM agreement for several years. Force reductions have resulted from the implosion of the Russian military, most particularly in the Far East, rather than controlled demobilisation or redeployment. They are in any case far less than the radical cuts envisaged when negotiations began. Moreover, the 1997 agreement excludes significant assets such as strategic missile forces, long-range aviation and naval deployments. No Border Guard reductions have been specified. According to Rodionov, 'Russian army groups currently in the Far East will remain there'.[62] Comments such as these did little, however, to stop the liberal Russian press bemoaning the 1997 agreement as a strategic mistake.[63]

Demarcation

Immediately after the collapse of the Soviet Union, border demarcation appeared within reach. In seeking the Supreme Soviet's ratification of the 1991 Russian–Chinese border agreement on 13 February 1992, then Foreign Minister Kozyrev argued that it did not 'envisage any alteration of today's borderline on land' nor 'any [Russian] territorial concessions'.[64] Following Chinese ratification, the Russian Foreign Ministry stated that 'the whole borderline between Russia and China ... except for its western section and three islands in the eastern one' was settled. In 1993, a Russian–Chinese Joint Border Demarcation Committee began its deliberations, with completion envisaged within five years. Further progress was made on 3 September 1994, when agreement was reached between the Russian and Chinese Foreign Ministers on the 55km western section of the border. At the same time, Jiang and Yeltsin witnessed a protocol covering joint navigation guidelines for Chinese shipping using the Tumen River. Since then, the two sides have issued a series of statements pledging to complete demarcation on time and in full accord with the 1991 arrangement. On 24 June 1996, these agreements were supplemented by deals between Russia, China and Mongolia preparing for final demarcation of the three countries' border intersections.[65]

As with trade ties, these developments conceal a wider fragility. Despite Russian Foreign Ministry confidence, the 1991 and 1994 deals did not cover all disputed areas. Agreement in 1991 was reached by omitting three islands – Bolshoy Ussuriisk and Tarabarov at the confluence of the Amur and Ussuri rivers near Khabarovsk,

Map 3 *Sino-Russian Border Disputes*

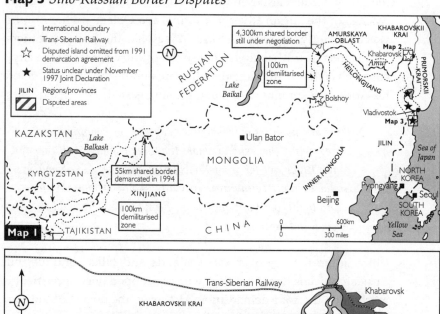

Map 1 legend:
- ·—·— International boundary
- ···· Trans-Siberian Railway
- ☆ Disputed island omitted from 1991 demarcation agreement
- ★ Status unclear under November 1997 Joint Declaration
- JILIN Regions/provinces
- ▨ Disputed areas

4,300km shared border still under negotiation

100km demilitarised zone

55km shared border demarcated in 1994

100km demilitarised zone

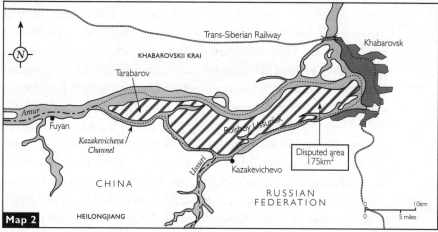

Trans-Siberian Railway

Disputed area 175km²

Disputed area 300 hectares

the site of border clashes in the late 1960s, and Bolshoy in the upper reaches of the Argun River in Chitinskaya Oblast – whose return was adamantly opposed by Russian regional and military leaders. The islands near Khabarovsk house the country homes of the city's élite; Yeltsin has made clear that they are non-negotiable. Just before his April 1996 summit with Jiang, Yeltsin insisted:

> There are instances in which we can agree to no compromises. For example, the issue to whom the three islands ... in the Amur River not far from Khabarovsk and the ... Bolshoy island in the Argun River in Chita should belong. With regard to this our position remains firm: the border should be where it lies now.[66]

China is keen to recover these islands and talks continue, but Russian officials hope that they will be dropped once agreement is reached on the 1991 demarcation. However, the details of the 1991 accord have proved troublesome, providing the basis for nationalist campaigns such as that by Nazdratenko. Although the precise principles by which disputed areas were to be demarcated have never been made public, basic elements and disputed areas are well known. Gorbachev broke the stalemate in 1986 by agreeing that the basis for demarcation should be 'the middle of the main navigable channel in navigable streams or the middle of the river in non-navigable streams'.[67] The 1991 agreement enshrined these principles and provided for the Joint Border Demarcation Committee to determine the national status of the hundreds of disputed islands in border rivers. At least 11 areas have proved contentious, but as a result of Nazdratenko's campaign, three areas between 2km- and 10km-square in the Khankaiskii, Ussuriiskii and Khansanskii districts have attracted the greatest attention.

Nazdratenko recruited regional representatives within the Demarcation Committee, arranged for Cossak units to be placed on disputed sections of the border and encouraged regional and federal Duma intervention. Regional opposition increased as both Nazdratenko and his counterpart in Khabarovskii Krai, Ishaev, secured positions on Russian negotiating delegations. Nonetheless, arguments over the economic and strategic value of the land to be returned met with little sympathy from the Russian Foreign

Ministry. In place of the prime agricultural and hunting grounds described in the regional press, the Ministry repeatedly labelled any land that may be handed over as worthless. Claims that concessions over the Tumen River could potentially confer access to the Sea of Japan are also dismissed. Although they would enable China to gain navigation rights over part of the river, North Korea, which holds the last stretch before it flows into the Sea, has been reluctant to grant similar access.

Yeltsin first offered a year's delay so that the region could put its case to the Demarcation Committee. China has also compromised. The boundary area containing the graves of Cossak soldiers has been redrawn and joint economic development of at least one disputed island in Chitinskaya Oblast has been discussed. However, contentious issues can no longer be comfortably finessed.

In preparing for the April 1996 summit, Yeltsin issued statements and decrees requiring strict conformity with the 1991 agreement and promising that demarcation would be complete by the end of 1997. In mid-1997, with Primorskii Krai in economic crisis, Yeltsin attempted to strip Nazdratenko of his powers. Finally, during a summit between Yeltsin and Jiang in Beijing in November 1997, the two leaders declared the border dispute resolved.

However, the summit concealed Russian and Chinese differences over border demarcation. Although Yeltsin and Jiang pronounced disputes at an end, no precise details of a final demarcation were released, no mention was made of the Tumen River, and the islands omitted from the 1991 agreement were again excluded. In the short term, this appears to be the best arrangement. Yeltsin has avoided risking his political legitimacy by insisting on an agreement which might see land being returned to China. Beijing in turn has effectively accepted the strength of Russian regional opposition. In the long term, it remains unclear whether competing Russian and Chinese claims have been laid to rest.

As long as Russia prefers to resist reaching a final solution; regional politicians such as Nazdratenko remain in power; and two-way trade is moribund, tensions between the select few who stand to benefit from closer ties, and the wider public and regional politicians who oppose fully normalised cross-border relations, will continue to expose the weakness at the heart of Russia's China policy.

chapter 3

Central Asia and Mongolia

Chinese and Russian interests have long clashed in the Central Asian states of Kazakstan, Kyrgyzstan and Tajikistan, and in Mongolia. The Sino-Soviet split compounded tensions between the two: China revived its claims to sections of the Kazak and Kyrgyz borders, and to some 33,000km^2 of Tajikistan. The Soviet Union exerted pressure on northern China through a massive military build-up along the Central Asian border and stationed forces in Mongolia within striking distance of Beijing. Moscow also fuelled separatist sentiment in the Chinese border province of Xinjiang by granting special privileges to ethnic Uighurs (the dominant minority in Xinjiang) resident in Soviet Kazakstan and Kyrgyzstan. China in turn developed ties with Pakistan, armed the *mujahedin* in Afghanistan during the 1980s and demanded Soviet withdrawal from Mongolia as a precondition for Sino-Soviet normalisation.

With the decline of Russian influence in the region since 1991 and the emergence of inexperienced new governments, the scope for continued tensions would appear considerable. However, Russia and China's concern for domestic and regional stability have provided the basis for limited strategic accommodation in Central Asia. This understanding has not resulted from Russia's efforts to develop an élite political partnership, but from the evident advantages to both sides. This process has enhanced both countries' role in the region and extracted important concessions from Mongolia and the new Central Asian states.

The peoples of Central Asia and Mongolia have traditionally turned to Russia for support against China, giving Moscow a distinct advantage over Beijing.[1] However, the collapse of Soviet power allowed China to fill the economic and strategic vacuum. The Soviet Union fell before border agreements could be signed, leaving the reluctant new states of Central Asia with the prospect of negotiating directly with Beijing. After the withdrawal of Soviet/Russian forces from Mongolia in 1992, the country was left with only 20,000 troops to cover its 4,500km border with China.[2] As in the Russian Far East, an early boom in cross-border trade collapsed amid local press complaints of poor-quality Chinese goods and hints of illegal immigration.[3] Cross-border ethnic and linguistic ties complicated the situation. According to Chinese and Soviet censuses, Xinjiang is home to 1.1m ethnic Kazaks, 375,000 Kyrgyz and 7.2m Uighur. The Uighur, Turkic-speaking Muslims, are now a minority in Xinjiang (49%) as a result of internal Han Chinese colonisation.[4] A further 266,000 Uighur live in Kazakstan and Kyrgyzstan.[5]

Russia's increasingly strident conception of its regional interests since late 1992 has had immediate consequences for Central Asia. As Kozyrev explained in October 1993, Russia would not countenance 'losing geopolitical positions that took centuries to conquer'.[6] Moscow sought a continued stake in the region's economic development, particularly exploitation of fossil-fuel resources, protection of ethnic Russians and the promotion of stability as a buffer between Russia's vulnerable southern rump and the Middle East and South Asia. These demands became more insistent in the light of conflicts in Nagorno-Karabakh, Chechnya and Tajikistan, the former Soviet south's 'arc of crisis'.

It has been argued that, with considerable economic gains at stake, China will increase its involvement in the region at Russia's expense, either strategically or economically. Central Asia and Mongolia will thus become the arena in which Sino-Russian strategic tensions are most likely to be played out.[7] One Russian analyst has warned that China is 'moving toward a leading position in the struggle for influence in the post-Soviet era'.[8]

Domestic and Regional Stability

Despite past antagonism, however, China and Russia have found common ground. Although their concerns are distinct, the two countries have achieved a *modus vivendi* which has formed the basis for Russia's interest in China as a long-term strategic partner.

For all the tensions engendered by the Sino-Soviet split, the massive military build-up reinforced both countries' sense of national integrity. Movement across what had long been porous borders was controlled, as was ethnic, religious and linguistic friction. The sudden collapse of the Soviet Union challenged both states' sense of security. Russia lost its traditional borders – and with them the bulk of its defences – and faced a series of actual and potential separatist movements across its southern underbelly. It feared the spread of Islamic fundamentalism within the former Soviet republics and a spill-over of the conflicts in Tajikistan and Afghanistan.

Russia and China have found common ground

Similarly, the retreat of Soviet power in Central Asia and full Mongolian independence exposed China's minority regions of Xinjiang and Inner Mongolia to ethnic independence movements and to Islamic and Buddhist activism. In the aftermath of the communist coup in Moscow in 1991, then Chinese Vice-President Wang Zhen toured Xinjiang, advising a 'steel wall to safeguard socialism and the unification of the motherland'.[9] The virtual collapse of the Tajik state since 1992 (under pressure from Islamic fundamentalists linked to Afghanistan) and renewed fighting in Afghanistan during 1997 heightened Chinese concerns. Gun- and drug-smuggling from Afghanistan and northern Pakistan into Xinjiang are a further cause for concern.

Nationalist and religious activists used the newly independent Central Asian states as a base for anti-Chinese activities. Since 1992, Uighur congresses culminating in calls for an end to repression in Xinjiang have been held in Kazakstan and Kyrgyzstan, despite the protests of Chinese officials.[10] Two Uighur organisations, the East Turkestan Committee and the Uighurstan Organisation of Freedom, emerged from a Kazak congress in June 1993 that attracted over 4,000 delegates.[11] Uighur activists in Xinjiang also developed links with their brethren in Central Asia, Turkey and Germany, disseminating news of minority dissidence both within and outside China. More open frontiers allowed Mongolian and Uighur activists to seek refuge in the Central Asian border states during Chinese crackdowns. In 1992, an Uighur separatist group based in Kazakstan threatened to mount raids across the border.[12]

Outside powers have fuelled fears of strategic and political instability in Central Asia. During the early to mid-1990s, Iran, Pakistan, Saudi Arabia and Turkey sought to build influence in the region. The reportedly oil- and gas-rich states of Kazakstan and Turkmenistan were the specific targets, but the largely Muslim and Turkic population of Central Asia meant that all the new states were viewed as vulnerable. With ethnic and linguistic ties throughout Central Asia and Xinjiang, Turkey promoted a secular pan-Turkic band of influence stretching from the Bosporus to China, and from 1991 invested in developing cultural, educational and infrastructure links. Ankara's proposed oil and gas pipeline linking Central Asia to Turkey and Europe, forming the backbone of this new region, would exclude Russia from development of the region's energy resources. Tehran and Islamabad threatened a more explicitly Islamic influence, prompting Western analysts to predict an unstable future marked by Iranian-style fundamentalism or a contest between Iranian and Turkic influences.[13]

More recently, Russian conservatives have been concerned by Japanese and US economic and political interest in the region. Tokyo initially directed economic aid to the Central Asian republics in preference to Russia. The US has made clear its commitment to Central Asian sovereignty, free exploitation of Caspian Sea resources and security links, including Central Asia's participation in NATO's Partnership for Peace (PFP) programme. Kyrgyzstan embraced PFP to counter Russian pressure, while Kazakstan developed contacts with the US military, such as a 1997 arrangement for US P-30 *Orion* aircraft to undertake aerial surveys for the Kazak government.[14] The Russian nationalist press speaks conspiratorially of US infiltration in the area, even suggesting that the Voice of America radio station has used Kazakstan and Kyrgyzstan as a base for broadcasts into China.[15]

Faced with challenges to its position, Russia has found an effective ally in China and its overriding concern with maintaining regional and border stability. As Kozyrev explained when the concept of a partnership was first floated in January 1994: 'Beijing has a better understanding than certain Western capitals of the danger that Central Asia faces from religious extremism'.[16] Although China has made clear that it will not tolerate Russia treating Mongolia as within its sphere of influence, it has no such reservations *vis-à-vis* Central Asia.

China's concern with stability and appreciation of the limits of its power have ensured that Beijing

a shared concern with maintaining stability

works to preserve the regional status quo, a key element of which is recognising and preserving Russian dominance. China has repeatedly stressed that its efforts are 'not directed against any third party', emphasising its limited role in the region and the strategic importance of Russia's presence, and implicitly consenting to Russia's treatment of the former Soviet borders as its own.[17] Beijing has supported Russia's view that the conflict in Tajikistan should be resolved by the CIS and has recognised the benefits of the Russian troop presence on the Tajik–Afghan border.

Central Asian fears of Islamic and ethnic activism have reinforced regional understanding of Russian and Chinese interests. A July 1996 article in *Kazakstanskaya Pravda* argued that China's good-neighbour policy had assuaged fears of its intentions and undermined 'the radical opposition, which uses the China factor as a source of anxiety for criticism of the peaceable policy of the Kazakstani leadership and a destabilisation of the situation in Kazakstan'.[18] Analyst Harlan Jencks concludes:

> The PRC [People's Republic of China] and the five Central
> Asian governments, in effect, have formed a latter-day "holy
> alliance" to maintain the political status quo – preventing
> ethnic and religious separatism anywhere in the region.[19]

China's desire to promote stability is a key factor in prompting Russian leaders and analysts to view Beijing as a strategic partner.[20] Russian supporters of partnership see it as a means to stabilise the southern and eastern Russian periphery. Moscow believes that Beijing can help in resisting the 'Western, and particularly the Turkish, advances in Central Asia and the Caspian Oil Basin', and 'provide Moscow with a lever on Pakistan, obliging it to rein in the Afghan Islamists and prevent the destabilisation of

Tajikistan'.[21] Press reports claim that Chinese diplomats in Islamabad have sought assurances from the Pakistani government to that effect.[22] Russia has attempted to invoke the twin threats of NATO expansion to China's borders (through Central Asia's participation in the Organisation for Security and Cooperation in Europe (OSCE) and PFP) and Islamic fundamentalism in Afghanistan and Tajikistan to draw China – at least superficially – into its preferred strategic understanding.

Economic Interests

The balance between Russian and Chinese economic interests in Central Asia and Mongolia is more delicate than that between their political concerns. Russia has taken an aggressive stance, exerting pressure to ensure its participation in major resource projects on favourable terms, and to marginalise rivals such as Turkey. Some analysts predict that China's growing investment in the region, particularly in Kazakstan, will inevitably lead to heightened competition with Russia. Russian Far Eastern politicians and analysts have complained that Chinese development of rail and land links with Central Asia is undercutting the economic viability of Russian Eurasian transport links. Concern has also been expressed over planned oil and gas pipelines from Kazakstan to China.

There is no doubt that China's economic success and determination to upgrade trade ties is attractive to Central Asia and Mongolia.[23] China has sought to boost trade and establish major infrastructure projects to facilitate contacts and revive the 'silk road' trans-continental routes.[24] China and Kazakstan have set up an investment commission, and China, Kazakstan, Kyrgyzstan and Pakistan signed a transport accord in late 1996.[25] The Chinese authorities speak of an economic corridor with highways, airlines and fibre-optic cables, and claim that 18,000 cooperative projects and 22.5bn yuan in trade have been agreed along the rail line.[26] Plans for this 'golden road' are matched by Chinese proposals for an 'oil bridge' linking China, Central Asia, Russia, the Middle East, Japan and Korea.[27] Chinese companies have also secured agreement to assist Mongolia in developing its oil and gas resources, and China has expressed interest in two ambitious Central Asian oil-pipeline plans. The first would link Turkmenistan with China and Japan; the second will run from Kazakstan through the Tarim Basin in Xinjiang to China and Shanghai. Prime Minister Li signed a formal protocol outlining plans to build the Tajik pipeline in May 1994, although full development will largely depend on whether the Tarim Basin proves commercially viable.[28]

China's economic interests in Kazakstan grew in 1997. In June, the China National Petroleum Corporation (CNPC) bought a 60% stake in Aktobemunajgaz, one of the country's main oil companies.[29] Two months later, Li signed what President Nursultan Nazarbayev termed the 'contract of the century' to develop an oil and gas field at Aktyubinsk in western Kazakstan, and to build two pipelines, one stretching 3,000km to China, the other 250km to the Turkmen border and on to Iran.[30]

Despite these developments, China's influence should not be overstated. In opening economic relations with Central Asia, Beijing aims to boost domestic growth, to lessen its dependence on Middle Eastern oil and to increase internal stability. The Xinjiang authorities have promoted development to counter political discontent, and the region's importance in China's plans has increased. Contacts across the border have been permitted, partly to highlight the gap in living standards between the impoverished former Soviet republics and the relatively prosperous Xinjiang.[31] However, because China's overriding goal remains domestic stability, Beijing has been careful to include Russia in its plans for regional development. It has refrained from providing grant aid, insisting that it wishes equitable economic relations in the region – not dependence or a sphere of influence. Chinese investment is largely confined to the immediate border region with Kazakstan. Chinese-Kazak trade has grown from $373m in 1992 to $497m in 1996; Kazak exports to China grew four-fold in the same period. By contrast, Russian-Kazak trade reached $5.1bn in 1996.[32] Chinese Defence Minister Haotian in October 1997 announced increased military cooperation, but this is likely to be confined to exchanges related to border security. In June 1997, Haotian's Kazak counterpart, Mukhtar Altynbayev, insisted that his government was unlikely to buy *matériel* from China.[33] Beijing has yet to make – and may be unable to afford – the level of investment required if it is to wield significant influence in the region, or undermine Russia's position.[34]

In addition, any return to more overt Sino-Russian rivalry is likely to occur in a more multilateral environment than previous

Table 5 *Russian and Chinese Trade with Central Asia, 1992–1996*

(US$m)

	Russia				China			
	Exports to	Imports from	Total two-way	Balance	Exports to	Imports from	Total two-way	Balance
Kazakstan								
1992	–	–	–	–	245	128	373	117
1993	–	–	–	–	189	239	428	-50
1994	1,828	1,815	3,643	13	153	179	332	-26
1995	2,922	2,493	5,415	429	83	287	370	-204
1996	2,342	2,771	5,113	-429	36	461	497	-425
Kyrgyzstan								
1992	172	94	266	78	16	28	44	-12
1993	–	–	–	–	19	59	78	-40
1994	–	–	–	–	11	56	67	-45
1995	105	114	219	-9	27	3	30	24
1996	175	135	310	40	8	36	44	-28
Tajikistan								
1992	–	–	–	–	2	1	3	1
1993	84	63	147	21	11	–	11	–
1994	61	46	107	15	5	1	6	4
1995	136	95	231	41	–	6	6	–
1996	74	79	153	-5	1	6	7	-5

Source IMF, *Direction of Trade Statistics Yearbook* (various years)

periods of competition. Russia and China are unlikely to have a free hand in the region, even if they succeed in restraining Turkish and Iranian influence. Once the Central Asian states begin to implement some of their more ambitious projects, they will become competitors with China for Western investment. Chinese-funded infrastructure will eventually link Central Asia with Europe, ultimately reinforcing the region's independence. Central Asia has in any case resisted excessive dependence on either China or Russia, seeking outside capital and security ties. Mongolia has also courted aid and investment: donors, led by Japan, had by 1995 pledged $765m in development aid, supplemented by $10.8m from the US to further 'strategic interests and democracy'.[35] According to Mongolian Presidential Adviser L. Galbagrakh, his country lies 'between two giants, therefore our cooperation with the United States is very important from the point of view of security as well as our progress toward democracy'.[36]

Normalisation

Russia and China have played to regional fears of the 'giants' to extract maximum concessions in normalisation negotiations. Kyrgyz Foreign Minister Roza Otunbayeva made the dilemma explicit in February 1996, explaining that 'our future survival will depend on how far we succeed in becoming the conduits of interests in this direction [China] or the other [Russia]'.[37]

Moscow has exploited this uncertainty to bolster its position as the region's security umbrella, and to ensure that the Central Asian states do not pursue policies that may prompt an assertive Chinese response. In September 1992, Russia signed an accord with Central Asia to adopt a common approach to China, including continued adherence to Soviet treaties and negotiations and a common CIS position on talks with Beijing.[38] Despite bilateral meetings and agreements, border and demilitarisation deals have been negotiated in the 'four-plus-one' framework, with Russia heading the CIS states. Moscow has also tied Central Asia into its security agenda. On 15 May 1992, a collective-security treaty was signed in Tashkent by Russia, Kazakstan, Kyrgyzstan, Uzbekistan and Armenia, giving the Russian High Command 'effective control over military activities in these states' and discouraging them from looking elsewhere for strategic support.[39] Bilateral treaties were also concluded with Kazakstan and Kyrgyzstan in May and June 1993.

China has used the promise of normalised relations, regular diplomatic summits, demarcation and security ties to increase border controls and to constrain Uighur activists based in Kazakstan and Kyrgyzstan. Beijing moved quickly to establish diplomatic ties with the new Central Asian states at the beginning of 1991; by the end of 1993, each head of state had visited Beijing. Li's 1994 tour was followed in 1996 by a visit by Jiang Zemin to Kyrgyzstan, Turkmenistan and Uzbekistan. This approach has been increasingly surefooted. Bilaterally, China signed border agreements and gave non-aggression guarantees to Kazakstan in 1994 and to Kyrgyzstan two years later.[40] Chinese officials hope that bilateral border negotiations will be completed by the end of the century. Contentious areas have been excluded from these bilateral accords, and demarcation of the Chinese–Tajik border has been deferred until order is restored in Tajikistan.[41] At the same time, Beijing has pressed ahead with the 'four-plus-one' negotiations over border demilitarisation.

China has registered protests with the Kazak and Kyrgyz authorities over separatist agitation. In the process, Chinese officials have stressed the threat to all border countries should violence in Xinjiang worsen or the province attempt to secede.[42] Beijing has also exploited diplomatic successes with Russia and the Central Asian states to move directly against Uighur activists. Before the April 1996 CBM agreement, Kazakstan and Kyrgyzstan signalled their understanding of China's interests in Xinjiang and promised to move against cross-border agitation. As soon as the CBM agreement was signed, China launched an apparently massive crackdown. Chinese officials denied opposition claims that over 18,000 Uighurs had been arrested in border villages, but did admit to detaining several thousand.[43] Between 22 April and the end of May 1996, Beijing banned Islamic books and cassettes and the construction of new mosques. In addition, it stepped up border controls and established 'quick reaction forces' to be deployed against resistance fighters in the region. As Lowell Bezanis concludes:

From the clockwork way in which the crackdown proceeded,
it appeared Beijing had planned it in advance and was only

*waiting for signals of approval from its neighbours to the
west ... Meanwhile, the Russian, Kazakh and Kyrgyz press
have remained conspicuously quiet about the issue.*[44]

In the face of escalating Uighur activism, including a series of
bombings in Beijing itself, China continued these security
crackdowns throughout 1997. Kazakstan has refused to discuss
suggestions of an Uighur autonomous region, while Kyrgyzstan has
registered no Uighur political party.[45]

In the same way, China and Russia played on Mongolia's fear
of encirclement to further their own agendas. China ended
Mongolia's attempts to cultivate closer ties with Taiwan in April
1994 by offering a nuclear non-targeting agreement in exchange for
Ulan Bator's acceptance of the one-China policy.[46] Russian diplomats
have hinted that only Moscow can help Mongolia to balance
relations with China in the long term.[47]

Beijing and Moscow have therefore achieved internal-security
goals along with their desired border arrangements. Nevertheless,
because this pressure has been exerted by normalising relations, and
in an increasingly multilateral climate, there are limits to its
effectiveness. Despite Chinese protests, the Dalai Lama visited Ulan
Bator in September 1994; Inner Mongolian activists have found
refuge in Mongolia, and have staged protests outside the Chinese
Embassy.[48] In early 1997, Ulan Bator declared itself a sister city of
Taipei, lifting the freeze on Mongolian–Taiwanese relations.
Similarly, Chinese actions in Xinjiang have attracted adverse
commentary in the Central Asian press. Kazak and Kyrgyz leaders
have been reluctant to submit to Chinese pressure to crack down on
Uighur activism, preferring to stress the benefits of economic
cooperation.[49] Neither country has curtailed Uighur activism to the
extent that Beijing would like.[50] Nazarbayev's emphasis on Kazak
ethnicity and his pursuit of contacts with China's Kazak population
have also irked Beijing.[51]

Partnership or Accommodation?

Central Asian stability is a common goal of Russia and China; their
policies towards the region and each other are mutually supportive.
However, there is little evidence that shared concerns have led to

overt coordination or partnership. Russia and China have signed an intelligence-sharing agreement that presumably covers Central Asia and Afghanistan. But relations are best described as suspended competition rather than active cooperation or a diplomatic framework to enhance strategic interests.

Russia's interest in developments in Central Asia is deeper than that of China. Although a spill-over of violence or activism from Central Asia or Afghanistan is a concern, Beijing would be reluctant to intervene across its borders. Martha Brill Olcott notes that 'Chinese sovereignty ... may depend as much on Beijing's ability to influence events across its borders as it does on controlling events within'.[52] But that would require a fundamental Chinese policy shift which is unlikely in the foreseeable future. Nor does China face economic challenges to the same degree: for many in Russia, Western oil and gas deals threaten to undercut the country's economic and political role. Pipeline routes are critical to Russia's future influence in the region. This disparity limits the opportunities for a more overt strategic understanding.

shared concerns but no partnership

The Central Asian states have demonstrated a marked preference for stability over democracy, cracking down on domestic dissent and discouraging pan-Turkic or Islamic sentiment. Outside competitors seeking influence have found far less fertile ground than originally expected. The reality of Central Asian life and the Soviet Union's secular state have left little taste for Islamic ideology, while *Shi'a*-Muslim Iran's failure to bridge the divide with mostly *Sunni* Central Asia further limits Tehran's appeal. US opposition has also thwarted Iranian attempts to play an independent role. Turkey has yet to find the financial resources to sustain its economic-development plans, and its conflict with separatist Kurds and the war in Nagorno-Karabakh have frustrated efforts to promote regional pipeline deals.[53]

The relative success of Russia and China's normalisation strategies in Central Asia and Mongolia begs comparison with the difficulties they have faced in pursuing their bilateral agendas. Russian leaders see a closer political partnership with China as a means of stemming their declining economic and strategic control, and of fending off other potential competitors. But, without a coordinated pursuit of normalised cross-border ties, the effect is a disjointed and insubstantial arrangement of limited lifespan. Moreover, Russia's attempts to deal with China in isolation in order to freeze the status quo – at least temporarily – in its favour carry considerable risks.

In Mongolia and Central Asia, however, shared concerns have allowed relations to progress more smoothly. Behind the talk of 'new' security arrangements, and Russian hopes of more active cooperation with China, both countries have individually played to the region's long-standing fears of their larger neighbours. Under the guise of multilateralism in the 'four-plus-one' framework, a series of essentially bilateral agreements has been made under which Moscow and Beijing have pledged to respect Central Asian sovereignty. In return, the Central Asian states have in effect declared their support for Russia and China's internal-security agendas.

chapter 4

Asia and Beyond

Until the end of the 1980s, Chinese–Soviet tension throughout North
and South-east Asia made itself felt in regional rivalries ranging
from Indo-China to the Korean Peninsula. Since the end of the Cold
War, however, Russia's influence has virtually collapsed, while
China's has grown. By seeking a strategic partnership with China,
Russia hopes to reinforce what influence it retains, regain its
standing in the UNSC and create a geopolitical balance to its often
fractious relations with the West. In doing so, Moscow risks
supporting Chinese military modernisation and other developments
that may pose a direct challenge to the West and, in the long term, to
its own security.

Moscow's sweeping goals and China's rise as an Asian power
make Asia the best test of the scope and substance of strategic
partnership. It is the region in which, theoretically, this relationship
could directly challenge Western interests. However, to date, partnership has done little to enhance Moscow's leverage in sensitive
areas of Western concern. While Russian arms sales to China are a
significant complication, they have yet to reach critical levels. Major
domestic realignments – particularly in China – are required before
the Sino-Russian relationship is capable of posing a more direct
challenge to the West.

A Strategic Partnership?

Relations between Russia and the 'East' are central to Russia's
Eurasianist and realist strategies of courting China as a political

partner. In theory, Russia's determination to extend its relationship with China challenges Western interests in Asia and in international organisations such as the UNSC. Russia's concerns about its declining influence and about US dominance have grown with its exclusion from key regional bodies such as the Korean Economic Development Organisation (KEDO), the four-party Korean Peninsula Talks between the two Koreas, China and the US, the Asia-Pacific Economic Cooperation (APEC) forum and the Asia–Europe Summit (ASEM). Russian leaders view China as their only diplomatic ally in the region, citing Beijing's support for Russian bids for APEC and ASEM membership and its – albeit more ambiguous – commitment to Russia as an Asian power.

China's interests are far less sweeping. It seeks Russian weaponry and adherence to the 'one-China' policy, but is wary of Russian attempts to develop alliances, has resisted coordinated action and is sceptical about Russian economic prospects, particularly in Asia. Nonetheless, China prefers to be seen as part of a loose grouping, rather than a sole objector, in regional and international fora. Russia's willingness to support Beijing and its residual influence in Korea and Vietnam are useful. Despite Russian talk of an 'Eastern option', Sino-Russian interests in Asia intersect on a case-by-case basis that is by no means evidence of substantive partnership.

Taiwan

The price of closer ties with Taipei has been strict adherence to Beijing's one-China policy, a move which cost Russia its initially promising relationship with Taiwan.[1] Before his December 1992 trip to Beijing, Yeltsin affirmed Russian recognition of the mainland as the sole Chinese state, and pledged that relations with Taiwan would remain unofficial. Russia did not criticise China during the March 1996 Taiwan Strait crisis, and made its support for Beijing explicit during the April 1996 summit.

Moscow seems to have devoted little time to assessing the risks in siding with the mainland. The Foreign Ministry has dismissed Taiwanese concerns over arms sales to China, claiming that since Russia does not recognise its independence, Taipei has no right to complain. Russian arms-industry officials assert that sales of Su-27 fighter aircraft or the mooted sale of two *Sovremennyy* destroyers will not affect the regional balance, despite the fact that China's original Su-27 purchase in 1991 helped to trigger Washington's decision to sell 150 F-16 fighters to Taiwan in 1992. Russian analysts such as Pavel Felgengauer suggest that Russia could harness the 'arms race' across the Taiwan Strait to its advantage:

> *For the foreseeable future, China will need Russian military technologies more than ever ... The sale of Russian-made fighters, submarines, advanced and long-range [missiles] ... could become not only a way for our hapless military–industrial complex to preserve jobs and earn money, but also the start of a long-range strategic partnership and a new balance of forces in Asia that would favor Russia.*[2]

Russian nationalists have explicitly advocated aiding China's military development in the Taiwan Strait, including providing Signals Intelligence (SIGINT) facilities and real-time satellite imagery which 'would increase the effectiveness of Chinese operations against the US 7th Fleet'.[3]

Nevertheless, Russia will not tolerate forceful reunification of Taiwan with the mainland.[4] Such a move would fuel Russian fears of China as a long-term threat, and would place enormous pressure on relations with the US.[5] Russian diplomacy suggests a recognition of the need for greater balance in Moscow's approach to the China–Taiwan issue. Although committed to the 'one-China' policy, Moscow has not abandoned hope of closer informal ties with Taiwan, by 1997 Russia's fourth largest trading partner in Asia. In December 1996, it was revealed that Russia had established a joint commission in Taipei to increase economic and cultural cooperation; Russian diplomats announced in March 1997 that agreement had been reached on direct air links. According to one high-ranking Russian diplomat, 'diversified unofficial Russia–Taiwan relations are not at variance with our official policy. Moreover, they are in our interests'.[6]

The Korean Peninsula
Russia and China have parallel interests on the Korean Peninsula, not least preventing the spread of nuclear weapons. Both countries

tried to reposition themselves towards the end of the Cold War by cooling relations with their erstwhile ally Pyongyang and developing closer ties with Seoul. In November 1992, Yeltsin announced that Russia would abandon or modify the 1961 Soviet–North Korea Treaty, particularly Article I which promised Russian assistance in the event of conflict. Bilateral relations declined steadily, culminating in South Korean President Kim Young Sam's visit to Moscow in June 1994, during which he and Yeltsin declared a 'constructive and mutually complementary partnership'.[7] China was more cautious, preferring to maintain ties with Pyongyang while recognising Seoul.

Parallel interests have thus been pursued in different ways, and have therefore not resulted in a unified approach to the Peninsula's problems. Russia responded robustly to North Korea's announcement in March 1993 that it

*no unified approach
to the Korean Peninsula*

intended to withdraw from the Nuclear Non-Proliferation Treaty (NPT). Moscow suspended all assistance to Pyongyang's nuclear programme and backed US demands that the regime comply with International Atomic Energy Agency (IAEA) inspections and rejoin the NPT. China by contrast worked quietly to prevent nuclear-weapon development without abandoning North Korea.[8]

Russia's decision to side with the US did little to further its long-term interests. In early 1994, Kozyrev warned that the Korean Peninsula was effectively part of Russia's sphere of influence and that Moscow 'would not consider measures that do not follow from its direct participation' in attempts to resolve its problems.[9] Yet by mid-1994, Russia had been sidelined by the US, its proposal for an eight-party settlement rejected in favour of the bilateral US–North Korea Framework Agreement, signed in October 1994. In early 1996, four-party talks between China, the two Koreas and the US began. Russia laid the blame for this marginalisation squarely on the US and on Kozyrev's support for US and South Korean goals. As *Pravda* commented:

> *Russia happened to be a chessman sacrificed by Washington
> while playing a diplomatic gambit on the Korean peninsula.*

It happened as if Russia and its interests in Northeast Asia
had disappeared ... If it is true that the Korean peninsula is
the gate to Northeast Asia, this gate is closed for Russia.[10]

Russia was also outmanoeuvred by China. By balancing its
links with North and South Korea, China 'was able to retain leverage
in dealing with the North Korean question in the international
community'.[11] From mid-1994, Russia tried to adopt a similar
position. It proceeded with debt-for-arms deals with the South while
renegotiating the Soviet–North Korea Treaty. Moscow also increased
official contacts with the Peninsula in the apparent hope that the
Sino-Russian strategic partnership would enhance its influence on
Korean issues. In April 1997, during a speech to the Chinese
National Defence University, Rodionov warned that 'Russia ...
would not stand apart' in the event of war on the Peninsula, a
statement described by *Kommersant Daily* as amounting to 'a pledge
on Moscow's part to side with the North Korean–Chinese bloc in the
event of any problem'.[12] Beijing also indicated its interest in Moscow's support and involvement. In 1994, China and Russia worked
together to prevent international sanctions against Pyongyang.[13]

Yet China has little desire to see Russia play a full role.
Russia's exclusion from the four-party talks leaves Beijing as the
only player able to speak for the North, while retaining strong ties
with the South. Korea was the only major issue not included in the
Joint Communiqué issued after the April 1996 summit and the
Statement on International Affairs that followed Jiang and Yeltsin's
1997 summit, suggesting disagreement between Moscow and
Beijing. Russia is left to recycle the Soviet Union's proposal for
'radical' troop cuts on both sides of the border and for replacing US
forces with soldiers from a neutral country, while also reducing its
original eight-party framework to six to include itself and Japan,
along with the four current parties.[14] However, Russia's economic
interests in South Korea – its third largest trading partner in Asia –
preclude mischief-making.

Sino-Russian ties have therefore done little to alter the
situation on the Korean Peninsula. Their significance could increase
were the US–North Korea Framework Agreement to collapse, or if
North Korea were to implode. In either event, Russia would seek to

reassert its interests but, with China and the US in dominant positions, Moscow would face an unpalatable choice between enhanced Chinese or US influence over a united Peninsula.[15]

Japan

While the Korea issue illustrates the limited prospects of the Sino-Russian partnership in Asia, Moscow's overtures to Tokyo undermine the credibility of implicit threats to side with China against Western interests. Russia's relationship with China was initially intended to reflect an explicit choice against closer relations with Japan, confirmation of the impasse over the Kuril Islands/Northern Territories and a widespread assumption in Russia and Japan that the two were no longer economically compatible. Russia's decision to court China at the expense of ties with Tokyo gave Beijing greater regional influence and, if maintained in the long term, would limit the ability of the major North-east Asian powers to counter an aggressive China.

Nevertheless, it has become clear that Russia is not courting China at Japan's expense. Russia's strategic partnership has coincided with a marked thaw in relations with Tokyo.[16] In early 1996, Vladivostok hosted the first Japanese naval visit since the 1920s; high-level official Russian visitors to Japan have expressed their desire to revive ties. Emphasising Russia's policy of developing relations with China and Japan in parallel, Foreign Minister Primakov coupled a November 1996 visit to Beijing with a trip to Tokyo, where

Russia is not courting China at Japan's expense

he apparently discussed progress over the Kuril Islands. Following the visit, Russia reduced its garrison to 3,500 troops and pledged further cuts. During his March 1997 State of the Nation address, Yeltsin expressed his hope that relations with Japan would improve, mentioning the Kurils directly, and Russia pressed its proposal that the islands be developed jointly with Japan.[17] A basic accord governing joint fishing rights around the islands was signed in July 1997, with Primakov hinting that final agreement was at hand.[18]

Underlying the thaw in relations is an apparent shift in Tokyo towards developing ties at a political, rather than bureaucratic, level, and Yeltsin and Primakov's commitment to balancing Russia's relations with Asian powers. In April 1996, Yeltsin and Japanese Prime Minister Ryutaro Hashimoto met (the first such meeting in three years); in May 1997, Rodionov became the first Russian Defence Minister to visit Tokyo. In July 1997, during the Group of Seven (G-7) summit in the US, Yeltsin and Hashimoto agreed to informal meetings at least once a year; Moscow offered to de-target Russian missiles directed at Japan and expressed support for Tokyo's bid for permanent membership of the UNSC. First Deputy Prime Minister Boris Nemsov visited Tokyo for a second bilateral meeting on trade and economic issues in June 1997, promising to accelerate joint economic development. Finally, Yeltsin and Hashimoto held a long-awaited summit in Russia in early November 1997 in which they set 2000 as the date by which they intended to complete a peace treaty.

The upturn in Russo-Japanese relations highlights the distance between Russia and China in their Asian security interests. During his May 1997 visit, Rodionov suggested tripartite co-operation between Japan, Russia and the US in ensuring Asia-Pacific security, including military exercises. Rodionov likened relations between the three countries to those of 'partners'.[19] Primakov has suggested that Russia's vision of a multipolar world would include a larger Japanese role.[20] Russia has reportedly briefed China on progress in its ties with Japan, but Rodionov's comments recognise the legitimacy of the US–Japan Security Treaty and emphasise that Russia is more comfortable than China with the United States' Asia-Pacific presence. Russia's marginalisation and history of multilateral security arrangements predispose it to the US-influenced security arrangements from which China has repeatedly shrunk.

Regional Security

Russia and China's involvement in the Association of South-east Asian Nations (ASEAN) Regional Forum (ARF) illustrates their divergent attitudes towards multilateral security in Asia. Stephen Blank accuses Russia of peddling 'indefeasible schemes for collective and joint security' in Asia, and of following China's lead in South-east Asia by proposing security initiatives which 'conform solely to China's security desiderata and "swindle" ASEAN into accepting a one China policy, rather than dealing with ASEAN's concerns'.[21]

Moscow's overtures to Beijing have hinted to that effect: during an April 1997 visit to China, Rodionov claimed that it was 'practically impossible to guarantee security in Asia and the Pacific' without the active involvement of China and Russia, and that the two 'must pursue a concerted policy, come out with joint initiatives to deepen a constructive dialogue in the military–political sphere in the region'.[22] Rodionov suggested that such consultations 'should focus on the development of a system of notification about major exercises, the limitation of the scale and duration of exercises, the mutual renunciation of exercises and manoeuvres in sea straits'.[23] In December 1996, Rodionov suggested that bilateral relations between Russia and China, Japan and the US, and the US and Russia should be 'tied into a single knot'.[24]

Insofar as these proposals question the pre-eminent role of the US in Asia-Pacific security, they offer China diplomatic benefits. Russia has promoted the CBM and demilitarisation agreements signed in 1996 and 1997 as a new security model applicable to the whole of the Asia-Pacific region, and has held briefings on them for numerous countries. India's December 1996 agreement with China was modelled on the five-country CBM. However, China has no interest in seeing Russia's initiatives progress further. Rodionov's security proposals are little more than a resurrected version of Gorbachev's model for a collective regional-security system. As with the Korean Peninsula, Russia's Asian diplomacy holds little direct appeal for Beijing since it depends on the 'great-power' initiatives which were effective during the 1980s, but carry little weight without Soviet military power. China does not want to see Russia raise its profile on regional-security issues, particularly in the multilateral manner that Moscow has proposed. Sino-Russian accommodation is therefore a mix of cooperation and mischief-making limited by Russia's marginalisation and China's preference for unilateral power balancing.

The United Nations

Russia and China's implicit threats to cooperate in the UNSC suffer from a similar lack of credibility. Russian support was crucial in defeating censure of China by the UN Human Rights Commission in Geneva in 1995. Russia and China also opposed economic sanctions against North Korea in 1994. Both countries have repeatedly lobbied to lift sanctions against Iraq and have indicated concern over peacekeeping policy, emphasising that operations should be sanctioned by the UNSC. As the 1997 Statement on International Affairs explains: 'We believe that the international organisation must be a guarantor of peace and security for all countries, that dual standards should not be applied to peacekeeping operations under its mandate'.[25] These statements reflect China's heightened concern over possible international intervention in its troubled minority regions, such as Tibet or Xinjiang, and Russia's desire to secure UN approval for its peacekeeping operations in the former Soviet Union.

However, China resists granting Russia a role in Korean Peninsula discussions, and is therefore reluctant to allow UNSC involvement. Russia's other strategic relations, most obviously with India, also reduce the possibility of wide-ranging cooperation. As part of its efforts to resuscitate ties, Russia has promised to support New Delhi's position on disputed Kashmir in the UNSC, and has backed India's bid for permanent Council membership. Neither development is likely to coincide with China's interests as a close ally of Pakistan.

Russian Arms Sales

Russia's arms sales to China are the most significant factor in assessing the two countries' relationship in Asia. China's priorities are air defence and naval power, particularly in relation to Taiwan.[26] Russia has vigorously defended the legitimacy and propriety of its arms sales in the teeth of Western criticism. Rodionov was unapologetic: 'I must make it clear that such technical cooperation is one of the directions that the development of Sino-Russian relations is taking at the inter-government level'.[27] At the same time, former Deputy Foreign Minister Aleksandr Panov insists:

> We don't want this cooperation to upset the balance of military forces in the region. We are not promoting cooperation in the domains that could harm our national interests. Moreover, all our international commitments are being observed. This cooperation is transparent.[28]

Russian and Chinese officials also claim that arms sales are defensive in nature and do not include latest-generation equipment.[29] However, the Russian arms industry's aggressive targeting of the Asian market has weakened government restrictions on technology transfer. According to Aleksandr Koltelkin, Director of the weapons-export corporation Rosvooruzhenie:

> *If previously the Soviet Union did not deliver, as a rule, the newest models of arms to other countries, today Russia sells modern, high-tech models. Also, these deliveries are occurring simultaneously with the introduction of these weapons systems in Russia's armed forces. This is an important difference of Russia's export policy from US policy. The United States often sells other than the best weapons systems abroad, and most often sells either used arms or arms which have been in the arsenal for many years.*[30]

As a result, the possible scope and consequent implications of Russia's reported sales to China have attracted widespread concern. Japan and Taiwan have objected to Russia's sale of Su-27s and *Kilo*-class submarines.[31] In 1995, the US cautioned Russia and Ukraine after rumours surfaced that the two had discussed with China the sale of SS-18 missile technology. US Secretary of Defense William Cohen noted that the reported sale of two *Sovremennyy*-class destroyers equipped with supersonic SS-N-22 anti-ship missiles designed to counter US *Aegis*-equipped ships posed 'a threat to our forces'.[32] The destroyer deal – thought to be part of a larger transaction worth $8–10bn – follows US involvement in the Taiwan Strait in March 1996. If cemented, the sale would enable the Chinese Navy to pose a far more credible threat to Taiwan, and would act as a deterrent should the US again intervene on Taipei's behalf.[33]

According to Western analysts, the Russian defence industry resists central control and makes sales, including to China, despite foreign- and defence-policy experts' concerns and in contravention of international agreements such as the Missile Technology Control Regime (MTCR).[34] A 1995–96 Su-27 licence deal was concluded independently of the authorities, reportedly to gain funding for a next-generation Su-37.[35] Critics have thus charged Russia with abetting China's irredentist agenda, fuelling arms proliferation in South Asia, and heightening a regional arms race in East Asia by offering the PLA offensive weaponry and technology transfers.[36] US

Table 6 *Chinese Arms Orders and Deliveries, 1995–1997*

Equipment	Type	Units	Supplier	Order	Delivery Date	Comment Date
Inter-continental ballistic missile	DF-31/41		Domestic	1985	1998	Development begun 1985
Submarine-launched ballistic missile	JL-2		Domestic	1985	2003	Development
Maritime patrol aircraft	radar	8	UK	1996		Searchwater to be fitted to Y-8
Airborne early warning aircraft	IL-76	4	Israel	1997		
Fighter, ground-attack	F-10		Domestic	1989	2003	Development; requirement for 300
Fighter, ground-attack	Su-27	72	Russia	1990	1995	Licensed production for further 150
Training aircraft	K-8		Collab.	1987		With Pakistan
Main battle tank	Type-90-II		Domestic	1990	1997	Development of Type 85IIM; trials 1996
Armoured personnel carrier	Type-90	2,000	Domestic	1990	1995	Family of 12 armoured fighting vehicles; 400 delivered 1996
Landing platform helicopter		1	Domestic	1996	2000	
Destroyer with area surface-to-air missile	*Sovremennyy*	2	Russia	1997		
Defence mobilisation ship		1	Domestic		1997	
Frigate	*Luhu*-class	3	Domestic	1991	1996	Second of class commissioned in 1996
Submarine	*Song*-class	3	Domestic	1985	1996	
Submarine	*Ming*-class	6	Domestic	1992	1996	1 delivered 1996
Submarine	*Kilo* 636	4	Russia	1993	1995	Deliveries to 1998
Nuclear-fuelled ballistic-missile submarine	Type 094	1	Domestic	1985	2000	Development; to carry JL-2 SLBM
Nuclear-fuelled submarine with dedicated non-ballistic missile launchers	Type 093	1	Domestic	1985	2002	Similar to Russian *Victor 3*

Source IISS, *The Military Balance 1997/98*

conservatives demand that President Bill Clinton's administration oppose the sale of the destroyers and other 'destabilising' weaponry – if necessary by limiting aid to Russia. Conservatives have also called on Clinton to sell submarines to Taiwan and to upgrade missile systems in the Seventh Fleet.[37]

These concerns outstrip actual sales and may exaggerate the breakdown in government export controls. Sales of Tu-22 *Backfire* long-range bombers and Su-35 fighters have reportedly been blocked by the Russian Foreign Ministry.[38] At least three factors suggest that Russian arms sales to China are unlikely to grow at the pace alarmist critics suggest. First, there is a fundamental tension between Russia's preferred off-the-shelf sales and China's goal of achieving indigenous defence production. Despite concern over technology transfer, Beijing's insistence on developing its own production capabilities, and preference for upgrading weapons systems itself, will continue to slow the pace of modernisation and extend technology-transfer negotiations. China has reportedly bought two basic versions of the *Kilo*-class submarine and Su-27, either to upgrade them itself or to gain access to key technologies for

Table 7 *Arms Deliveries to China, 1987–1996*

Year	Value	
1987	841	(constant 1995 US$m)
1988	537	
1989	599	
1990	345	
1991	332	
1992	1,398	
1993	603	
1994	267	
1995	725	
1996	1,500	

Note 1996 figures are provisional
Source IISS, *The Military Balance 1997/98*

indigenous variants. It will take many years before either aim is achieved. Second, the Sino-Russian defence market is unstable. Russia's sales to China, although important, do not guarantee the long-term survival of its defence industry. Conversely, China will diversify supplies when it can and sees its purchases of Russian equipment as a means of pressuring Western countries, especially France, to resume sales. Finally, the arms-sale relationship remains a fundamentally *business*, rather than *strategic*, partnership.[39] Russia has yet to achieve the same level of cooperation and cordiality with China as it has with India, and is unlikely to do so in the foreseeable future. The coincidence of Russian eagerness to sell and Chinese need to buy has not resulted in the large-scale purchases anticipated by many Western and Russian critics.

Asia's Changing Balance of Power

Nonetheless, Russia's arms sales raise broader questions which cut to the heart of China's rise as a great power in the Asia-Pacific, the possible impact of Sino-Russian relations on the regional balance of power and Russia and China's long-term commitment to stable bilateral relations. The dispute with the Soviet Union and Moscow's military build-up constrained China's ability to realise its great-power ambitions until the late 1980s. Gorbachev's decision to seek *rapprochement*, and the subsequent collapse of Soviet and Russian military strength, allowed China to consolidate its position as the pre-eminent power in mainland East Asia.[40] Russia's once-significant edge is being blunted: Moscow's economic and military base continues to shrink and, although still possessing highly advanced weaponry, the military's poor performance in Chechnya has undermined its credibility. China's influence, by contrast, is growing throughout North and, especially, South-east Asia.[41]

The Yeltsin government's defence and strategic cooperation with China, combined with a commitment to lessening military pressure along their joint border, highlights the most troubling aspect of China's rise – its alteration from an inward-looking, continental power to a growing regional player on its southern and eastern maritime fringe.[42] As one Pentagon analyst has explained: 'By securing its land relationships and tidying up immediate borders, China can pursue longer-term interests, which lie increasingly in the sea lanes' which are of direct strategic concern to the

West.[43] Sino-Russian partnership could potentially influence China's development in one of two ways.

A Sino-Russian Bloc?

Russia could help to consolidate China's rise. Behind both countries' conception of their relationship is a common desire to counter-balance US power.[44] The April 1996 summit invoked the backdrop and imagery of the Cold War strategic triangle; the meeting took place less than a week after a visit to Moscow by Clinton and within a month of the reaffirmation of the US–Japan alliance.[45] Some Russian strategists believe that Russia has a historic opportunity to exploit Sino-US tensions to foster ties with China and the US simultaneously:

> *military cooperation with Moscow enables Beijing to bargain confidently with the US and to get what it needs – including economic assistance – from America. Naturally, such a role constitutes very valuable political capital for Russia and it can be exploited. But it can also be lost if we conspicuously turn our relations with China into something secondary, into a bargaining chip in dealings with the West (even if only in word).*[46]

Russian supporters of closer ties insist that any irredentist ambitions are oriented to the south, and that Moscow can exploit Beijing's need for a 'reliable rear'. 'Under these conditions, China is very much in need of stability and friendly regimes on its north-western borders.'[47]

Yet such debates do not necessarily reflect the practice of Russian or Chinese bilateral diplomacy. Neither country has opted for a relationship that directly challenges Western interests, and it is unclear why either should seek to do so. Trade ties with the US far outweigh bilateral trade and command the greatest attention in both countries. For all the talk in Russia of a Sino-Russian axis, there remains a widespread awareness that 'the idea of seeking allies in the East ... is unrealistic, futile and dangerous':

> *But the plan, popular in our country, of using the 'reserve option'– an alliance with the Eastern giants if entry into*

*Europe doesn't work out – is primitive and illusory in and of
itself. In real life, everything is more complicated. Alliances
are built gradually and over long periods of time, and are
based not on the wishes of individual public-affairs writers,
but on economic realities.*[48]

For many, the foundations of a triangular balancing strategy
evaporated with the end of the Cold War. China has recoiled from
Russian attempts to portray their relationship as an alliance or bloc.
By the April 1997 summit, with NATO enlargement a foregone
conclusion, Russian officials sought to step back from earlier claims
that relations with China offered an explicit counter to the West. In
both countries, significant domestic realignments are needed before
the relationship becomes an overt challenge to Western – specifically
US – power.

Russian analysts and political leaders are also aware of the
implications should China adopt a more assertive stance in the
future.[49] Russian analyst Dmitry Trenin argues that, over the next 10–
15 years, 'the relative weakness of Russia and strength of China will
become clearer' and that 'it is this reality that Russian leaders should
bear in mind today'.[50] Aleksey Arbartov warns:

*The hope of 'placating' China with huge shipments of arms
and military technology, securing its border trade, and taking
advantage of the mounting friction in Chinese–Japanese
relations is just as naive and anti-historical as it is dangerous
for Russia. Nothing will keep China from turning to the
north at the convenient time if its access to the east and south
is blocked by strong forces.*[51]

Strategic Triangle Revisited?

Alternatively, Russia and China might revert to a more extensive
and explicit power-balancing in North-east Asia. In many respects,
both are already doing so. Behind the talk of partnership, their
emphasis on multipolar, equidistant relations reflects mutual
distrust and an attempt to develop bilateral ties while expanding
links with the US, Japan and others. Were China to adopt a more
aggressive regional stance, Russia might lean in favour of the US
and Japan. Many Western analysts assume that unresolved tensions,

and Russia's fear of Chinese power, make this the most likely long-term outcome.[52] To many Western critics, Russia should view China not as a partner, but as a long-term challenge; Western policy-makers, in turn, can either rely on bilateral tensions to limit Russia's tilt towards China, or actively encourage a more distant Sino-Russian relationship.

Such discussion is misplaced. Fears of Russian over-dependence on China have yet to be realised. Undoubtedly, in the event of heightened tensions between China and Taiwan, South-east Asia or the US, a neutral, acquiescent or weakened Russia would be harmful to US interests. Equally, given that all countries concerned wish to avoid a return to outright conflict or Cold War-level tensions, improved Russian relations with Japan are crucial. But now is not the time to encourage such a shift in Russia's overburdened and fragmented foreign policy.

It is important to recognise the largely benign outcome of the present relationship for three reasons. First, debate over Russia's role as a counter-balance to China only inflames nationalist and anti-US sentiment in Russia. Conservatives portray their country as caught between allegiance to the US on the one hand and to China on the other. Western appeals for caution over future Chinese action against Taiwan or in the South China Sea are viewed as a 'trap' to force Moscow to act as a 'second front' against Beijing.[53] Many Russians suspect that those who criticise Russia's overtures to China do so to undermine the limited, but profitable, relationship with Beijing.

Second, although the Russian government's strategy of cultivating a strategic partnership with China is flawed, superficial and has reached its natural limits, it does not follow that this policy actually endangers Russia's interests. Russian and Western critics of the strategy assume that Moscow's overtures strengthen China's hand, and that confrontation is inevitable in the long term. In reality, the regional balance sheet is shifting in China's favour for a range of reasons which have very little to do with decisions made in Moscow or the Russian Far East.

Third, behind the rhetoric of strategic partnership lies the original goal of stabilising long-term relations through normalised cross-border ties. This agenda entered a critical new phase in November 1997 after the Yeltsin government's attempts to defer further opposition to the border agreements and focus instead on maintaining stable cross-border ties. Establishing a 'normal' relationship remains an important bilateral objective. Rather than weakening Russian control of the Far East, a stable, legal regime governing the border, and economic ties with northern China, are fundamental to Moscow's management of the longer-term consequences of China's rise. As the newspaper *Segodnya* argued during the April 1996 summit:

> *The only possible concept of relations with China that would be useful to Russia is a complete normalization of these relations. Great powers are unable to maintain partnerships with one another simply because they do not know how: for them, a partner is always a younger brother. As for disarmament and arms control, this is a field of co-operation that will be of mutual interest for a long time to come in any political situation.*[54]

Sino-Russian normalisation is all the more important because those in Russia who oppose establishing legal borders and opening economic ties are essentially the same groups that oppose closer relations with Japan. It is only through a continued commitment to establishing normalised ties with both China and Japan that Russia can create the political relationships necessary for a more stable balance in North-east Asia.

conclusion

Russia and China's strategic partnership is unwieldy and imprecise. Weighed down by contradictory commitments, hyperbolic rhetoric and a wide variety of intersecting interests, the relationship is inherently and deliberately vague. Behind the talk of novel relations of global significance, Russia and China have been engaged since the mid-1980s in the painstaking process of negotiating a stable, normalised relationship, with demilitarised borders and open trade. Moves to develop a strategic partnership are best understood as a parallel and often incoherent effort to put gloss on this more fundamental – albeit less dramatic – process.

Normalisation and partnership are not mutually exclusive agendas. Much of what has been cited between 1996 and 1997 as evidence of enhanced strategic cooperation was anticipated as part of normalisation. The 1996 CBM agreement, generally hailed as the greatest achievement of the strategic partnership, was simply a by-product of the demilitarisation negotiations begun in 1989 by Gorbachev and Deng.

Nowhere is this sleight of hand more apparent than in Central Asia and Mongolia. Both China and Russia have exploited the normalisation process to gain agreement with the former Soviet states of Kazakstan, Kyrgyzstan and Tajikistan over their appropriate roles and interests. The 'four-plus-one' negotiating framework established to carry on demilitarisation negotiations after the collapse of the Soviet Union has allowed Russia to cement its military and strategic role in the region, while China has accepted that process in exchange for Central Asian promises to curtail ethnic and religious activism. Where a framework for continued normalisation negotiations is absent, for example in the Asia-Pacific and international organisations, the strategic partnership has failed to persuade even the participants. Although both countries share concerns over US 'hegemony', they have reached no understanding, nor do their interests converge. Despite their attempts to promote the 1996 CBM agreement as a model for regional cooperation in the Asia-Pacific, Russian and Chinese approaches to security in North and South-east Asia and in international organisations diverge sharply. China's pragmatism and determination to pursue an independent foreign policy mean that no coherent Sino-Russian anti-US posture will emerge.

The normalisation and partnership agendas do not always interact well because Russia and China's priorities do not coincide. Beijing attaches far greater importance to normalisation, Moscow to partnership. Since late 1993, Russia has sought political partnership over substantive normalisation. The Yeltsin government has attempted to harness élite relations to manage the deep domestic opposition to fully normalised borders and open economic relations. During the mid-1990s, this strategy gave the Russian government important breathing space, but emphasising partnership over normalisation carries risks. Russia and China's economic relationship remains unstable and limited; border negotiations have become protracted and fraught. The emphasis on partnership has encouraged the view in Russia that closer ties can be pursued without satisfying China's desire to finalise border agreements and open up trade. Stronger political relations allowed Russia at first to slow the pace of border negotiations to placate local opposition. However, these delays, and attendant insubstantial declarations of progress, reinforce the view popular in Russia that negotiations can only be finalised at the country's expense.

The April 1996 Sino-Russian summit was the high-water mark in this process of balancing partnership and normalisation. Russia and China portrayed a minor demilitarisation agreement as a substantive development, railed against US 'hegemony' and repeatedly invoked the imagery of the Cold War strategic triangle. At the same time, Russia pressed for access to major Chinese projects, while dragging out border negotiations. Were this still the dominant tone, the consequences would damage both countries' relations with Western powers and the prospects for long-term, stable bilateral ties.

Fortunately, although still dominated by high-level summitry, with presidential meetings in April and November, there were signs in 1997 of slightly cooled rhetoric and reduced expectations. This was a particularly welcome development for China, which succeeded in keeping negotiations on track while signalling its reluc- *an equal-but-distant* tance to be seen as a counter to *relationship* NATO expansion. In the short term at least, China appears set to secure its desired 'equal-but-distant' relationship. For Russia, 1997 marked a grudging recognition of the limits of the strategic partnership. While many Russian analysts still look to Beijing as a counter-weight to US power, it is clear that this is not a viable alternative. Although Russia's partnership with China is likely to be a constant in Russia's diplomatic vocabulary for the foreseeable future, it will probably be pursued with less ambition and self-delusion than has previously been the case.

Limited Sino-Russian partnership will remain couched in grandiose terms, but in practice there are few deals left that can easily be portrayed as major fruits of partnership. Relations will continue to involve difficult negotiations over borders and trade. Moscow and Beijing must return, privately at least, to building a stable, long-term relationship. That focus will be matched, however, by continued Russian arms sales to China. The arms-sales relationship may even become more important if Russian companies fail to secure high-profile contracts in other areas.

A limited partnership based on the normalisation process has two implications for Western policy-makers.

- First, policy-makers must prepare for a long-term Russian commitment to sell high-technology weapons to China. This will be a priority for both Moscow and Beijing. Sales have yet to reach levels that would justify the US sanctions that conservative critics have recommended, but Western governments may be confronted by Chinese purchases which clearly destabilise the regional status quo. The limits of acceptable

Russian arms sales must be clearly set and communicated to the Russian government.

- Second, Western policy-makers and analysts need to recognise the strategic implications of a limited Sino-Russian partnership grounded in a continuing commitment to normalisation and stable long-term ties. The US and other Western governments insist publicly that continued demilitarisation and border agreements further the interests of all countries concerned. But this view is often coupled with a belief that Russia and China will inevitably, and usefully, counterbalance each other. Many Russia specialists writing on the relationship also strongly believe that Moscow is endangering its long-term security by pursuing closer links with China, and that it will seek to counter-balance Beijing through deeper ties with the West, notably Japan. What is lacking is a perception of the parallel danger of poor future Sino-Russian ties, or of the benefits of a normalised, legal bilateral relationship.

Western policy-makers tend to view progress in Russo-Japanese or Russo-Chinese ties as mutually exclusive, yet at present they are reinforcing each other. Although the two relationships are traditionally promoted by competing sectors of the Russian Foreign Ministry, conservative and Far East politicians block progress in both.

Western governments and analysts need to make clearer to Russia the benefits of improved relations with China, and the position such relations occupy in a benign Asia-Pacific balance of power. Dialogue, even-handedness and sharp messages are the key. In particular, the West needs to signal its interest in a stable Sino-Russian border and in enhanced bilateral ties.

Ultimately, though, the future of the partnership is in Russia's hands. It is in a return to incremental resolution of local difficulties and an open economy, rather than presidential summitry or sweeping declarations of a new world order, that one of the key factors governing the long-term stability of mainland Asia will be determined.

notes

Chapter 1

[1] Lowell Dittmer, 'China and Russia: New Beginnings', in Samuel S. Kim (ed.), *China and the World: Chinese Foreign Relations in the Post-Cold War Era* (Boulder, CO: Westview Press, 1994), p. 97.

[2] Eric Hyer, 'The Sino-Russian Boundary Settlement', International Boundaries Research Unit (IBRU), *Boundary and Security Bulletin*, vol. 4, no. 2, Summer 1996, p. 90. Chinese historians have placed the amount of disputed territory at 1.5 million square kilometres. In practice, Chinese leaders pressed for the return of 35,000km^2 of land, 33,000km^2 of which lies in Tajikistan.

[3] Harry Gelman, 'The Soviet Far East Military Buildup: Motives and Prospects', in Richard H. Solomon and Masataka Kosaka (eds), *The Soviet Far East Military Buildup: Nuclear Dilemmas and Asian Security* (Beckenham: Croom Helm, 1986), p. 47.

[4] James Clay Moltz, 'From Military Adversaries to Economic Partners: Russia and China in the New Asia', *Journal of East Asian Affairs*, vol. 9, no. 1, Winter 1995, p. 162.

[5] Hung P. Nguyen, 'Russia and China: The Genesis of an Eastern Rapallo', *Asian Survey*, vol. 33, no. 3, March 1993, p. 289.

[6] William Wohlforth, 'Refining Security: Russia's Intellectual Adjustment to Decline', *Harvard International Review*, vol. 19, no. 1, Winter 1996–97, p. 13.

[7] Yevgeny Afanasiev, 'Declaration Not a Rhetorical Document', *Rossiyskiye Vesti*, 25 April 1997, p. 1, translated in Foreign Broadcast Information Service (FBIS)-SOV-97-115, 28 April 1997.

[8] Sergei Kortunov, 'Russia: Objectives for Partnership with US Set', *Mirovaya Ekonomika i Mezhdunarodnyye Otnosheniya*, no. 7, pp. 70–78, 1 July 1996, translated in FBIS-SOV-96-209-S, 29 October 1996.

[9] Chikahito Harada, *Russia and North-east Asia*, Adelphi Paper 310 (Oxford: Oxford University Press for the IISS, 1997), pp. 50–51.

[10] Alexander A. Sergounin and

Sergey V. Subbotin, 'Understanding Sino-Russian Military Cooperation: A Source of Stability or Tension?', unpublished paper, Stockholm International Peace Research Institute (SIPRI), 1996, p. 9; Alexander Rahr and Joachim Krause, 'Russia's New Foreign Policy', *Arbeitspapiere zur Internationalen Politik 91* (Bonn: Forschungsinstitut der Deutschen Gessellschaft für Auswärtige Politik, 1995), p. 5.

[11] Wohlforth, 'Refining Security', pp. 11–13.

[12] Alexander Rahr, '"Atlanticists" versus "Eurasians" in Russian Foreign Policy', *RFE/RL Research Report*, vol. 1, no. 22, May 1992, p. 20.

[13] Ronald C. Keith, 'The Post-Cold War Political Symmetry of Russo-Chinese Bilateralism', *International Journal*, vol. 49, no. 4, Autumn 1994, p. 775.

[14] Rahr and Krause, 'Russia's New Foreign Policy', pp. 5–6.

[15] 'Major Events in Sino-Russian Relations in Recent Years', *Xinhua Domestic Service*, 1 September 1994, translated in FBIS-CHI-94-173, 12 November 1994.

[16] Ho Tan-chi, 'Inside Story on Yeltsin's Letter to Jiang Zemin, Russian Leaders' Recent Visits to Beijing', *Kuang Chiao China* (Hong Kong), no. 261, 16 June 1994, pp. 6–8, translated in FBIS-CHI-94-130, 12 November 1994.

[17] Keith, 'The Post-Cold War Political Symmetry of Russo-Chinese Bilateralism', p. 752.

[18] See *Beijing Review*, vol. 34, no. 21, 27 May–2 June 1991, pp. 7–12.

[19] Eugene Bazhanov, 'Russian Policy Toward China', in Peter Shearman (ed.), *Russian Foreign Policy Since 1990* (Boulder, CO: Westview Press, 1995), p. 172.

[20] Ustina Markus, 'To Counterbalance Russian Power, China Leans towards Ukraine', *Transition*, vol. 1, no. 17, 22 September 1995, pp. 34–37.

[21] Greg Austin, 'Russian Influences and Mutual Insecurity', in Stuart Harris and Garry Klintworth (eds), *China as a Great Power: Myths, Realities and Challenges in the Asia-Pacific Region* (Melbourne: Longman Australia, 1995), p. 114.

[22] See Samuel S. Kim, 'China in the Post-Cold War World', in Harris and Klintworth (eds), *China as a Great Power*, p. 48.

[23] Samuel S. Kim, 'Mainland China in a Changing Asia-Pacific Regional Order', in Bih-jaw Lin and James T. Myers (eds), *Contemporary China in the Post-Cold War Era* (Columbia, SC: University of South Carolina Press, 1996), pp. 286–87.

[24] Bazhanov, 'Russian Policy Toward China', p. 169.

[25] Austin, 'Russian Influences and Mutual Insecurity', p. 118.

[26] Quoted in Kim, 'Mainland China in a Changing Asia-Pacific Regional Order', pp. 286–87.

[27] Quoted in Austin, 'Russian Influences and Mutual Insecurity', p. 119.

[28] Ho Tan-chi, 'Inside Story on Yeltsin's Letter to Jiang Zemin'.

[29] 'PRC Declaration, Nuclear Missile Pact Summarized', *ITAR-TASS*, 3 September 1994, translated in FBIS-SOV-94-172, 3 September 1994.

[30] See Stephen Blank, 'Towards the Failing State: The Structure of Russian Security Policy', Conflict Studies Research Centre, Working Paper F56, November 1996, p. 2; Celeste A. Wallander, 'Coming into Focus: Understanding Russia's Security Interests', *Harvard*

International Review, vol. 19, no. 1, Winter 1996–97, pp. 14–15.

[31] David M. Lampton, 'China and the Strategic Triangle: Foreign Policy Continuity in an Age of Discontinuity' in Michael Mandelbaum (ed.), *The Strategic Quadrangle: Russia, China, Japan and the United States* (New York: Council on Foreign Relations Press, 1995), p. 85.

[32] 'PRC Declaration, Nuclear Missile Pact Summarized'.

[33] Pi Ying-hsien, 'The Dynamics of Sino-Russian Relations', *Issues and Studies*, vol. 32, no. 1, January 1996, p. 30.

[34] *Ibid.*, p. 24.

[35] Wohlforth, 'Refining Security', p. 57.

[36] Rahr and Krause, 'Russia's New Foreign Policy', p. 16.

[37] See Vasiliy Safronchuk, 'Key of Trust: What They Have Been Able to Open with it in Russian-Chinese Cooperation', *Sovetskaya Rossiya*, 26 April 1997, translated in FBIS-SOV-97-081, 29 April 1997.

[38] See 'Rodionov Identifies "Sources of Military Danger"', *Interfax*, 25 December 1996, in FBIS-SOV-96-249, 27 December 1996; 'Foreign Minister Rodionov Says Partnership with China a "Long Term Strategy"', *Interfax*, 14 April 1997, in *BBC Summary of World Broadcasts, The Former USSR* (SWB/SU) 2893 B/5, 15 April 1997.

[39] See, for example, Pavel Felgengauer, 'Russia and the Conflict in the Taiwan Strait: Moscow and Beijing in New Strategic Partnership', *Segodnya*, 13 March 1996, p. 5, translated in Current Digest of the Post-Soviet Press, vol. 49, no. 11, 10 April 1996, p. 10.

[40] Li Tzu-ching, 'CPC Thinks China and the United States Will Eventually Go to War', *Cheng Ming*, no. 235, May 1997, pp. 15–16, translated in FBIS-CHI-97-126, 7 May 1997.

[41] Zhang Linhong, 'The US Policy towards Russia in the Wake of the General Election There', China Institute for International Strategic Studies (CIISS) Journal, pp. 31–32.

[42] Jen Hui-wen, 'Sino-Russian Relations as Viewed from Internal Report', *Hsin Pao*, no. 18, translated in FBIS-CHI-96-129, 5 July 1996.

[43] Yegor Yakolev, 'Russia's National Interests: Interview with Yevgeny Primakov', *Obshchaya Gazeta*, 15 August 1997.

[44] 'A Breakthrough for Russian Foreign Policy on the Asian Front', *Rossiyskiye Vesti*, 24 April 1997, p. 1, translated in Current Digest of the Post-Soviet Press, vol. 49, no. 17, 28 May 1997, p. 1.

[45] Austin, 'Russian Influences and Mutual Insecurity', p. 120.

[46] See Zbigniew Brzezinski and Michael Oksenberg, 'The China Drift', *Washington Post*, 15 June 1997, p. C9.

Chapter 2

[1] Aleksandr Platkovsky, 'Our Home Makes Friends with Chinese Communist Party', *Izvestia*, 12 March 1997, p. 3, translated in Current Digest of the Post-Soviet Press, vol. 49, no. 10, p. 21, 9 April 1997.

[2] 'Russian Ambassador Comments on Bilateral Cooperation', *Xinhua*, 17 April 1996, translated in FBIS-CHI-97-113, 25 April 1997.

[3] Grigoriy Karasin, 'Russia–China: Road to Strategic Cooperation in the 21st Century', *Rossiyskiye Vesti*, 26 December 1996, translated in FBIS-SOV-96-250, 30 December

1996.

[4] Peter Kirkow, 'Regional Warlordism in Russia: The Case of Primorskii Krai', *Europe–Asia Studies*, vol. 47, no. 6, 1995, pp. 923–47, 925; James Clay Moltz, 'Regional Tensions in Russo-Chinese Rapprochement', *Asian Survey*, vol. 35, no. 6, June 1995, p. 515.

[5] Moltz, 'Regional Tensions', p. 520; 'Russian Far East & Siberia' in *Asia 1994 Yearbook*, Far Eastern Economic Review, December 1993, p. 197.

[6] Kirkow, 'Regional Warlordism', p. 924.

[7] Vladimir Portyakov, 'Are the Chinese Coming? Migration Processes in Russia's Far East', *International Affairs* (Moscow), vol. 42, no. 1, January–February 1996, http://home.eastview.com/ia/index.html.

[8] Tamara Troyakova, 'Regional Policy in the Russian Far East and the Rise of Localism in Primorskiy Krai', *Journal of East Asian Affairs*, vol. 9, no. 2, Summer 1995, p. 451.

[9] Rajan Menon, 'The Strategic Convergence between Russia and China', *Survival*, vol. 39, no. 2, Summer 1997, p. 105.

[10] Portyakov, 'Are the Chinese Coming?'.

[11] James Clay Moltz, 'Core and Periphery in the Evolving Russian Economy: Integration or Isolation of the Far East', *Post-Soviet Geography and Economics*, vol. 37, no. 3, March 1996, p. 185.

[12] 'Russia: "Illegal" Migrants from PRC Deported from Maritime Kray', *Rabochaya Tribuna*, 23 November 1996, p. 3, translated in FBIS-SOV-96-229, 27 November 1996.

[13] Portyakov, 'Are the Chinese Coming?'.

[14] Valentina Voronova, 'The Governor Said: Not an Inch!', *Obshchaya Gazeta*, no. 19, 11–17 May 1995, p. 8, translated in FBIS-SOV-95-112, 12 June 1995.

[15] 'Russian Far East & Siberia', p. 199.

[16] See Moltz, 'Regional Tensions', p. 521.

[17] James Cotton, 'China and Tumen River Cooperation', *Asian Survey*, vol. 36, no. 11, November 1996, pp. 1,086–1,101.

[18] Won Bae Kim, 'Sino-Russian Relations and Chinese Workers in the Russian Far East', *Asian Survey*, vol. 34, no. 12, December 1994, p. 1,074.

[19] Icksoo Kim, 'Tumen River Development and Economic Cooperation', *Asian Perspective*, vol. 19, no. 2, Autumn/Winter 1995, p. 88.

[20] Ludmila Zabrovskaya, 'The Tumanggang Project: A View from Primorie', *Far Eastern Affairs*, no. 1, 1995, p. 35.

[21] See Vladimir Shlapentokh, 'Russia, China and the Far East: Old Geopolitics or a New Peaceful Cooperation?', *Communist and Post-Communist Studies*, vol. 28, no. 3, March 1995, pp. 307–18; Alexei D. Voskressenski, 'The Perceptions of China by Russia's Foreign Policy Elite', *Issues and Studies*, vol. 33, no. 3, March 1997, pp. 1–20.

[22] Shlapentokh, 'Russia, China and the Far East', p. 313.

[23] Yegor Gaidar, 'The Russia of the 21st Century: Not the World's Gendarme, but an Outpost of Democracy in Eurasia', *Izvestia*, 18 May 1995, translated in FBIS-SOV-95-099, 23 May 1995, p. 22.

[24] Sherman Garnett, 'The Russian Far East in Sino-Russian Relations', Paul H. Nitze School of Advanced International Studies (SAIS), *SAIS*

Review, vol. 16, no. 2, Summer/ Autumn 1996, p. 6.
[25] Wallander, 'Coming into Focus: Understanding Russia's Security Interests', pp. 14–15.
[26] Ivan Shomov, 'China Ready to Embrace Russia', *Segodnya*, 25 March 1997, translated in Russian Information Agency (RIA), *Daily Review*, 25 March 1997, www.ria-novosti.com/ria_main.html.
[27] 'Russian Far East & Siberia', pp. 196–99.
[28] *Ibid.*, p. 197.
[29] Local economic statistics do not allow accurate assessments of border trade.
[30] Moltz, 'Regional Tensions',p. 522.
[31] Burnham O. Campbell, 'Prospects for Trade and Regional Cooperation', in Mark Valencia (ed.), *Russian Far East in Transition: Opportunities for Regional Economic Cooperation* (Boulder, CO: Westview Press, 1995), p. 19.
[32] Moltz, 'Regional Tensions',p. 523.
[33] Judith Thornton, 'Recent Trends in the Russian Far East', *Comparative Economic Studies,* vol. 37, no. 1, Spring 1995, p. 83; Judith Thornton, 'Structural Change in the Russian Far East: Implications for Trade and Factors Markets', *Atlantic Economic Journal*, vol. 24, no. 3, September 1996, p. 215.
[34] Moltz, 'Regional Tensions',p. 522.
[35] Nikolay Belyy, *Rossiyskiye Vesti,* 18 April 1996, translated in FBIS-SOV-96-113-S, 18 April 1996.
[36] *ITAR-TASS*, 8 August 1995, in FBIS-SOV-95-152, 8 August 1995.
[37] Speech by Jiang Zemin at the Institute of International Relations, Moscow, 3 September 1994, in Joint Publications Research Service (JPRS)-TAC-94-012-L, 3 September 1994.
[38] Vladimir Kuznechevskiy, 'Together into the Twenty-First Century. On the Results of the Russian-Chinese Talks', *Rossiyskaya Gazeta,* 30 June 1995, 1st ed., pp. 1, 7, translated in FBIS-SOV-95-126, 30 June 1995.
[39] Vsevolod Ovchinnikov, 'Northern Hong Kong: Free Economic Zone May Grow Between Cities of Zabaykalsk and Manchzhuriya. Will We Help?', *Rossiyskaya Gazeta*, 10 August 1996, p. 7, translated in FBIS-SOV-96-179-S, 13 September 1996; 'Sino-Russian Economic, Trade Region in Heihe Viewed', *Zhongguo Xinwen She*, 27 August 1996, translated in FBIS-CHI-96-169, 30 August 1996.
[40] 'Progress in Constructing Rail Link Between Tumen River Region and Russia', in SWB/FE 0460 WG/ 11/45, 6 November 1996; 'Siemens Provides Equipment for Sino-Russian Optical Cable', *Xinhua*, 22 February 1997, in FBIS-CHI-97-036, 25 February 1997.
[41] 'Border Fair Trade With Russia Increases', *Xinhua*, 11 March 1997, in FBIS-CHI-97-070, 13 March 1997.
[42] Y. Paniyev, 'Moscow and Beijing Have Determined New Priorities of Future Cooperation', *Delovoi Mir*, 1 July 1997, translated in RIA, *Daily Review,* 1 July 1997, www.ria-novosti.com/ria_main.html.
[43] Oleg Shchedrov, 'Russia, China to Bury Past during Yeltsin Visit', *Reuters*, 9 November 1997.
[44] Shih Chun-yu, 'New Type of Sino-Russian Partnership', *Ta Kung Pao,* 25 April 1996, p. A4, translated in FBIS-CHI-96-081, 25 April 1996; Sophie Quin-Judge, 'Common Cause: Russia and China Join Hands for Mutual Benefit', *Far Eastern Economic Review*, 8 May 1997, pp. 15–16.
[45] See 'Russian Firm to Compete in China's Aviation Market', *Xinhua*, 27 April 1996, in FBIS-CHI-96-083,

30 April 1996; 'Russia, China Study Project for Joint Airline', *ITAR-TASS*, 24 April 1997, in FBIS-SOV-97-114, 25 April 1997.

[46] 'Sino-Russian Partnership Has Entered New Stage', *Wen Wei Po*, 29 December 1996, p. A6, translated in FBIS-CHI-97-002, 29 December 1996.

[47] Sergounin and Subbotin, 'Understanding Sino-Russian Military Cooperation', p. 35; Bates Gill and Taeho Kim, *China's Arms Acquisitions from Abroad: A Quest for Superb and Secret Weapons* (New York: Oxford University Press, 1995), p. 53.

[48] Aleksey Baliyev, 'Great Friendship Growing Through Kalashnikovs', *Rossiyskaya Gazeta*, translated in FBIS-SOV-96-196, 5 October 1996; 'Russian Arms Exports to China', *Jane's Defence Weekly*, vol. 26, no. 19, 6 November 1996, p. 19.

[49] Andrey Krushinskiy, 'Words and Deeds: The Term "Friendship" has Returned to the Russian and Chinese Vocabulary', *Pravda*, 7 September 1994, p. 7, translated in FBIS-SOV-94-173, 7 September 1994.

[50] See 'Russia's Primakov on Developing Strategic Partnership', *Xinhua*, 18 November 1996, in FBIS-CHI-96-224, 18 November 1996.

[51] Lorien Holland, 'China Urges Improved Trade Ties with Russia as Fifth Summit Looms', *Agence-France Presse*, 8 November 1997.

[52] Stephen Blank, 'Why Russian Policy is Failing in Asia', *Journal of East Asian Affairs*, vol. 11, no. 1, Winter 1997, p. 296.

[53] Yevgeny Afanasiev and Grigory Logvinov, 'Russia and China: Girding for the Third Millennium', *International Affairs* (Moscow), nos.

11–12, 1995, p. 48; Pi Ying-hsien, 'The Dynamics of Sino-Russian Relations', *Issues and Studies*, vol. 32, no. 1, January 1996, p. 21.

[54] Robert Karniol, 'Treaty Between China and Russia in Sight', *Jane's Defence Weekly*, 18 September 1993, p. 8.

[55] Personal communication; Illya Vulavinov, 'Russia's Boundless Friendship with China', *Kommersant Daily*, 25 April 1997, p. 2, translated in Current Digest of the Post-Soviet Press, vol. 49, no. 17, p. 5.

[56] 'Russia and China Sign Pact to Avert Military Mishaps', *International Herald Tribune*, 13 July 1994.

[57] Ibid.

[58] 'Agreement Between the Russian Federation, the Republic of Kazakhstan, the Kyrghyz Republic, the Republic of Tajikistan and the People's Republic of China on Confidence Building in the Military Field in the Border Area', April 1996, unofficial translation, NAPSNet, www.nautilus.org.

[59] See 'Landmark Border Deal Signed', *South China Morning Post*, 25 April 1997; 'FBS Director Hails Accord on Arms Reduction Along Borders', *ITAR-TASS*, 26 April 1997, translated in FBIS-SOV-97-116, 29 April 1997; 'China No Military Threat to Russia for 15 Years', *Interfax*, 19 April 1997, in FBIS-UMA-97-109, 22 April 1997.

[60] 'Russia and China in Troop Agreement', *Reuters*, 24 April 1997.

[61] Natalia Pulina and Aleksandr Reutov, 'An Agreement Whose Preparation Began Back in the Time of the USSR was Concluded with the PRC Yesterday', *Nezavisimaya Gazeta*, 25 April 1997, p. 1, translated in Current Digest of the Post-Soviet Press, vol. 49, no. 17, p. 5.

[62] 'Rodionov Cites Course Toward PRC Strategic Partnership', *Interfax*, 14 January 1997, in FBIS-SOV-97-009, 15 January 1997.
[63] Aleksandr Chudodeyuev, 'Russian-Chinese Songs On the Essence of the Universe – The Country with the Most People Will Lead the Singing', *Segodnya*, 24 April 1997, pp. 1, 4, translated in Current Digest of the Post-Soviet Press, vol. 49, no. 17, 28 May 1997, p. 4.
[64] Yakov Zinberg, 'The Vladivostok Curve: Subnational Intervention into Russo-Chinese Border Agreements', IBRU, *Boundary and Security Bulletin*, vol. 4, no. 3, Autumn 1996, pp. 76–77.
[65] 'Border Agreements Signed with PRC, Mongolia', *ITAR-TASS*, 24 June 1996, translated in FBIS-SOV-96-123, 26 June 1996.
[66] Hyer, 'The Sino-Russian Boundary Settlement', p. 92.
[67] See Zinberg, 'The Vladivostok Curve', pp. 79–80.

Chapter 3

[1] See Martha Brill Olcott, 'Central Asia: the Calculus of Independence', *Current History*, vol. 94, no. 594, October 1995, p. 337.
[2] Bertil Lintner, 'Mongols Fear Hordes', *Far Eastern Economic Review*, 18 May 1995, p. 30.
[3] Frederica Moroni, 'A State in Transition: Security Issues in Kazakhstan', *International Spectator*, vol. 29, no. 4, October–December 1994, p. 46.
[4] Keith Martin, 'China and Central Asia: Between Seduction and Suspicion', *RFE/RL Research Report*, vol. 3, no. 25, June 1994, pp. 26–36, p. 28.
[5] Gudrun Wacker, 'China Builds Ties, Trade Across its Western Border', *Transition*, vol. 2, no. 17, 23 August 1996, p. 30; Lowell Bezanis, 'China Strikes at Uighur "Splittists"', *ibid.*, p. 35; Dru C. Gladney, 'The Muslim Face of China', *Current History*, vol. 92, no. 575, September 1993, p. 276.
[6] Quoted in Stephen Page, 'The Creation of a Sphere of Influence: Russia and Central Asia', *International Journal*, vol. 49, no. 4, Autumn 1994, p. 806.
[7] Bruce E. Elleman, 'Russian Policy in the Chinese Context' in Stephen Blank and Alvin Z. Rubenstein (eds), *Imperial Decline: Russia's Changing Role in Asia* (Durham, NC: Duke University Press, 1997), p. 109; Stephen Blank, 'Energy, Economics and Security in Central Asia: Russia and its Rivals', *Central Asian Survey*, vol. 14, no. 3, 1995, p. 396.
[8] Irina D. Zvyagelskaia, 'Central Asia and the Caucasus: New Geopolitics' in Vitaly Naumkin (ed.), *Central Asia and Transcaucasia: Ethnicity and Conflict* (Westport, CT: Greenwood Publishing Group, 1994), p. 133.
[9] J. Richard Walsh, 'China and the New Geopolitics of Central Asia', *Asian Survey*, vol. 33, no. 3, March 1993, p. 272.
[10] Martin, 'China and Central Asia', p. 29.
[11] Valentin Shishlevskiy, 'Kazakhstan: Profile of a Latent Central Asian Power', *Asian Defence Journal*, vol. 5, 1994, p. 24.
[12] Lillian Craig Harris, 'Xinjiang, Central Asia and the Implications for China's Policy in the Islamic World', *China Quarterly*, no. 133, March 1993, p. 118.
[13] Brill Olcott, 'Central Asia: the Calculus of Independence', p. 337.
[14] 'Russia Objects to Kazak Survey

by US Plane', *RFE/RL Newsline*, 1 July 1997.

[15] Aleksey Artemov, 'Central Asia: Playing on the Road', *Rossiyskaya Gazeta*, 18 January 1997, p. 11, translated in FBIS-SOV-97-019, 30 January 1997.

[16] See Robert Levgold, 'Russia and the Strategic Quadrangle' in Mandelbaum (ed.), *The Strategic Quadrangle*, p. 49.

[17] Martin, 'China and Central Asia', p. 31. Also see Page, 'The Creation of a Sphere of Influence', p. 802.

[18] 'New Stage on the Path of a Strengthening of the Republic of Kazakhstan's Geostrategic Positions in the Region', *Kazakstanskaya Pravda*, 8 July 1996, translated in FBIS-SOV-96-131-S, 9 July 1996.

[19] Harlan W. Jencks, 'The PRC's Military and Security Policy', in Lin and Myers (eds), *Contemporary China in the Post-Cold War Era*, p. 237.

[20] Walsh, 'China and the New Geopolitics of Central Asia', pp. 277–78.

[21] *Inside Russia and the Former Soviet Union*, 15 April 1996, p. 11.

[22] Roger Howard, 'Afghanistan: Taliban Offensive May Spark Cross-Border Reaction', *Jane's Defence Weekly*, 9 April 1997, p. 15.

[23] Martin, 'China and Central Asia', p. 30.

[24] 'CIS–China Exchanges', *Voice of Russia World Service*, Moscow, 1 February 1997, in FBIS-SOV-97-023, 1 February 1997; 'Chinese-Kazak Rail Cooperation Discussed', *Kazakstanskaya Pravda*, 25 January 1996, p. 2, translated in FBIS-SOV-96-028, 9 February 1996; 'Good Relations Between the Peoples and Industry Will Lead to Confidence and Prosperity', *Kazakstanskaya Pravda*, 25 February 1997, pp. 1–2, translated in FBIS-SOV-97-014, 4 March 1997.

[25] 'Good Relations Between the Peoples', pp. 1– 2; 'Deal with China, Central Asia on Highway Trade Reported', *PTV Television Network*, Islamabad, 13 October 1996, in FBIS-NES-96-200, 17 October 1996.

[26] 'Northwest China to Revitalize "Silk Road"', *Xinhua*, 26 March 1997, translated in FBIS-CHI-97-085, 27 March 1997.

[27] 'Experts Call for Pan-Asia Continental Oil Bridge', *Xinhua*, 16 June 1996, translated in FBIS-CHI-96-117, 18 June 1996.

[28] Rosemarie Forsythe, *The Politics of Oil in the Caucasus and Central Asia*, Adelphi Paper 300 (Oxford: Oxford University Press for the IISS, 1996), p. 48.

[29] 'Round-up on Ties with Kazakstan', *Xinhua*, 22 September 1997, translated in FBIS-CHI-97-266, 23 September 1997.

[30] 'PRC's Li Peng at Signing of $9.5 Billion Oil, Gas Deal', *Interfax*, 24 September 1997, in FBIS-SOV-97-267, 24 September 1997.

[31] Wacker, 'China Builds Ties, Trade Across its Western Border', p. 33.

[32] *Direction of Trade Statistics Yearbook, 1997* (Washington DC: International Monetary Fund, 1997).

[33] 'Chinese, Kazakh Defence Ministers Discuss Expanding Ties', *ITAR-TASS*, 4 October 1997, translated in FBIS-CHI-97-278, 5 October 1997; 'Kazakstan: No Intention of Buying Arms from China', *Interfax*, 16 June 1997, translated in FBIS-UMA-97-167, 18 June 1997.

[34] Walsh, 'China and the New Geopolitics of Central Asia', p. 281; Artemov, 'Central Asia: Playing on the Road'.

[35] Lintner, 'Mongols Fear Hordes', p. 30.
[36] Elleman, 'Russian Policy in the Chinese Context', p. 111; Lintner, 'Mongols Fear Hordes', p. 30.
[37] *Novaya Yezhednevhnaya Gazeta*, no. 5, 8–14 February 1996, p. 2, translated in FBIS-SOV-96-083-S, 29 April 1996.
[38] Martin, 'China and Central Asia', p. 30.
[39] Page, 'The Creation of a Sphere of Influence', p. 793.
[40] 'Joint Declaration of the People's Republic of China and the Republic of Kazakhstan', *Xinhua*, 5 July 1996, translated in FBIS-CHI-96-131, 9 July 1996.
[41] Wacker, 'China Builds Ties, Trade Across its Western Border', p. 33.
[42] 'Good Relations Between the Peoples and Industry', pp. 1–2.
[43] Bezanis, 'China Strikes at Uighur "Splittists"', p. 34.
[44] *Ibid.*
[45] 'Good Relations Between the Peoples and Industry', pp. 1–2; Bezanis, 'China Strikes at Uigher "Splittists"', p. 35.
[46] Elleman, 'Russian Policy in the Chinese Context', p. 113.
[47] *Ibid.*
[48] Lintner, 'Mongols Fear Hordes', p. 30.
[49] See, for example, 'Nazarbayev's Timely Trip to China', *OMRI Daily Digest*, no. 17, 24 February 1997.
[50] 'Separatist Chinese Muslim Leader Interviewed', *NTV*, Moscow, 12 October 1996, translated in FBIS-SOV-96-201, 17 October 1996.
[51] 'China, Kazakhstan Plot Huge Migration of Xinjiang's Ethnic Groups', *Chien Shao*, no. 37, August 1996, pp. 34–35, translated in FBIS-CHI-96-180, 17 August 1996.
[52] Martha Brill Olcott, *Central Asia's New States: Independence, Foreign Policy and Regional Security* (Washington DC: United States Institute of Peace Press, 1996), p. 36.
[53] Blank, 'Energy, Economics and Security in Central Asia', p. 387.

Chapter 4

[1] Leszek Buszynski, *Russian Foreign Policy After the Cold War* (Westport, CT: Praeger Publishers, 1996), p. 193.
[2] *Segodnya*, 13 March 1996, p. 15, translated in Current Digest of the Post-Soviet Press, vol. 48, no. 11, 10 April 1996, p. 10.
[3] Vladislav Shurygin, 'Interview with Anton Viktorovich Surikov', *Zavtra*, no. 14 (122), April 1996, p. 5, translated in FBIS-UMA-96-080-S, 25 April 1996.
[4] Alexei D. Voskressenski notes that only a 'marginal part of the Russian élite … will even tolerate forceful unification'. See Voskressenski, 'The Perceptions of China by Russia's Foreign Policy Elite', p. 17.
[5] Gennadiy Chufrin, 'Russia and the China–China Crisis', *Moskovskiye Novosti*, no. 12, 24–31 March 1996, translated in FBIS-SOV-96-085-S, 2 May 1996.
[6] *Interfax*, 13 March 1997, translated in FBIS-SOV-97-072, 15 March 1997.
[7] Alexandr Zhenin, 'Russia and Korean Unification', *Asian Perspective*, vol. 19, no. 2, Autumn/Winter 1995, p. 178.
[8] Eunsook Chung, 'Russia's Policy Trends Toward North Korea', *Vantage Point*, vol. 19, no. 11, November 1996, p. 37.
[9] Zhenin, 'Russia and Korean Unification', p. 180.
[10] *Ibid.*, p. 182.
[11] Chung, 'Russia's Policy Trends

Toward North Korea', p. 37.
[12] *Agence-France Presse*, 15 April 1997, in FBIS-CHI-97-105, 16 April 1997; 'Russia and China Prepared for Tough Cooperation', *Kommersant Daily*, 16 April 1997, p. 3, translated in Current Digest of the Post-Soviet Press, vol. 49, no. 15, 14 May 1997, p. 25.
[13] Personal communication, May 1997.
[14] 'Russia's Six-Party Peace Talks Proposal', NAPSNet, *Daily Report*, 19 June 1997, ftp://ftp.nautilus.org/napsnet.
[15] See Harry Gelman, 'The US and Russia's Far East Policy', in Blank and Rubenstein (eds), *Imperial Decline: Russia's Changing Role in Asia*, pp. 223–24.
[16] See 'Russian, Japanese Politicians Discuss Asia-Pacific Issues', *ITAR-TASS*, 30 June 1997, translated in FBIS-SOV-97-181, 2 July 1997.
[17] James Clay Moltz, 'Russia in Asia in 1996: Renewed Engagement', *Asian Survey*, vol. 37, no. 1, January 1997, p. 93.
[18] 'Primakov Addresses Japanese Journalists on Ties, US, Korea', *Interfax*, 16 July 1997, translated in FBIS-SOV-97-197, 17 July 1997.
[19] 'Rodionov Calls Relations with Japan, US Partnership', *Kyodo*, 16 May 1997, translated in FBIS-EAS-97-136, 19 May 1997; 'Tokyo Ready to Discuss Joint Russian–US–Japanese Exercises', *ITAR-TASS*, 18 July 1997, translated in FBIS-UMA-97-199, 22 July 1997.
[20] 'Primakov Addresses Japanese Journalists on Ties, US, Korea'.
[21] Blank, *Towards the Failing State*, p. 11; 'Beijing Rejects Grachev's Alliance Proposals', translated in Current Digest of the Post-Soviet Press, vol. 48, no. 20, 14 June 1995, p. 22; Xuewu Gu, 'China's Policy Towards Russia', *Aussenpolitik*, vol.

44, no. 3, 1993, p. 293; 'China Offers Accord to "Reassure" ASEAN', *Jane's Defence Weekly*, vol. 25, no. 25, 19 June 1996, p. 27.
[22] 'Further on Rodionov Elaboration on Areas of Cooperation', *Interfax*, 15 April 1997, translated in FBIS-SOV-97-105, 16 April 1997.
[23] *Ibid*.
[24] Ilya Bulavinov, 'Igor Rodionov Greeted Like Member of G-7 – For the First Time a Russian Defense Minister Pays an Official Visit to Japan', *Kommersant Daily*, 20 May 1997, p. 4, translated in Current Digest of the Post-Soviet Press, vol. 49, no. 20, 18 June 1997, p. 21.
[25] 'Further on Rodionov Elaboration on Areas of Cooperation'.
[26] See *The Military Balance, 1997/98* (Oxford: Oxford University Press for the IISS, 1997), p. 170.
[27] 'Russian Defense Minister Defends Arms Sales to China', *Agence-France Presse*, 15 April 1997, in FBIS-CHI-97-105, 16 April 1997.
[28] Andrey Varlamov and Andrey Kirillov, 'No Objections to Military Co-operation with the PRC Foreseen', *ITAR-TASS*, 4 January 1996, in FBIS-96-SOV-003, 5 January 1996.
[29] See, for example, 'Government Official: Military Sales to China will Boost Army Finances', *ITAR-TASS*, 12 December 1996, in SWB/SU/D2794/S1, 13 December 1996.
[30] Igor Khripunov, 'Have Guns will Travel', *Bulletin of the Atomic Scientists*, vol. 53, no. 3, May–June 1997, p. 50.
[31] 'Japanese General Cites Chinese Modernization', *Defense News*, vol. 12, no. 11, 17–23 March 1997, p. 2.
[32] 'Priority for Cohen is Top Personnel Recruitment', *Jane's Defence Weekly*, vol. 27, no. 4, 29 January 1997, p. 6.
[33] Bill Gertz, 'Pentagon Says

Russians Sell Destroyers to China', *Washington Times*, 10 January 1997, p. 1.

[34] See Blank, 'Why Russian Policy is Failing in Asia', pp. 284–85.

[35] Blank, *Towards the Failing State*, p. 9.

[36] See, for example, Richard D. Fisher, 'Dangerous Moves: Russia's Sale of Missile Destroyers to China', The Heritage Foundation, *Asian Studies Center Backgrounder*, no. 146, 20 February 1997, www.townhall.com/heritage/library/categories/forpol/asc146.html.

[37] *Ibid.*

[38] John Zeng, 'The New Sino-Russian Partnership: Su-27s the Icing on the Cake', *Asia-Pacific Defence Reporter*, vol. 22, nos. 5–6, May–June 1996, p. 21.

[39] See Sergounin and Subbotin, 'Understanding Sino-Russian Military Cooperation'.

[40] See Robert S. Ross, 'Beijing as a Conservative Power', *Foreign Affairs*, vol. 76, no. 2, March–April 1997, pp. 34–35.

[41] Garnett, 'The Russian Far East in Russian-Chinese Relations', p. 6; Gelman, 'The US and Russia's Far East Policy', pp. 231–32.

[42] Larry M. Wortzel, 'China Pursues Traditional Great-Power Status', *Orbis*, vol. 38, no. 2, Spring 1994, p. 160.

[43] Barbara Opall, 'China Widens Global Reach', *Defense News*, 27 January–2 February 1997, pp. 1, 19.

[44] See Vasily Pakin, 'Co-operation Behind Closed Doors, Iran Can Help Russia Create an Eastern Axis', *Kommersant Daily*, 12 April 1997, p. 4, translated in Current Digest of the Post-Soviet Press, vol. 49, no. 15, 14 May 1997, p. 26.

[45] Peter Rodham warns of 'a rapprochement ... that has disturbing geopolitical implications'. See Rodham, 'A New Russia–China Alliance?', *Los Angeles Times*, 25 March 1996, p. B5. According to Henry Kissinger, 'the [April 1996] communiqué represents nothing less than a declaration of independence by both Moscow and Beijing from the strategic triangle'. See Kissinger, 'Moscow and Beijing: A Declaration of Independence', *The Washington Post*, 14 May 1996, p. A15.

[46] Dmitry Kosyrev, 'China and the US Smile at Each Other – Beijing Benefits from Rivalry Between Moscow and Washington', *Nezavisimaya Gazeta*, 2 April 1997, p. 4, translated in Current Digest of the Post-Soviet Press, vol. 49, no. 13, 30 April 1997, p. 25.

[47] Felgengauer, 'Russia and the Conflict in the Taiwan Strait', p. 10.

[48] Vladimir Abarinov, 'Benefits of Alliance with China are Dubious', *Segodnya*, 13 March 1996, p. 5, translated in Current Digest of the Post-Soviet Press, vol. 48, no. 11, 10 April 1996, p. 12; Kosyrev, 'China and the US Smile at Each Other', p. 4.

[49] Aleksey Arbartov, 'Aleksey Arbartov Ponders Security Needs in the Late 1990s', *Mirovaya Ekonomika i Mezhdunarodnyye Otnosheniya*, July–September 1994, translated in FBIS-USR-94-129, 9 November 1994.

[50] See Quin-Judge, 'Common Cause', p. 16.

[51] Arbartov, 'Security Needs in the Late 1990s'.

[52] Sherman Garnett, 'Slow Dance: The Evolution of Sino-Russian Relations', *Harvard International Review*, vol. 19, no. 1, Winter 1996, p. 66; Rajan Menon, 'Japan–Russia Relations and North-east Asian

Security', *Survival*, vol. 38, no. 2, Summer 1996, p. 59.

[53] Lieutenant-General Valeriy Denetyev, 'RF [Russian Federation] Armed Forces Reform Strategy: A Specific Plan Must be Developed and Approved Based on Two Doctrines – Military and National Security', *Nevazismoye Voyennoye Obozreniye* (supplement to *Nezavisimaya Gazeta*), no. 7, 11 April 1996, pp. 1, 4, translated in FBIS-UMA-96-080-S, 11 April 1996; Andrey Ivanov, 'We Will Build Our Own Multipolar World', *Novoye Vremya*, nos. 17–18, 4 May 1997, pp. 22–23, translated in FBIS-SOV-97-103, 31 May 1997; Henry Trofimenko, 'US-Russian Relations in East Asia' in Blank and Rubenstein (eds), *Imperial Decline: Russia's Changing Role in Asia*, p. 256; Boris Zanegin, 'Kremlin Foreign Policy "Duplicity" Scored', *Zavtra*, no. 38, September 1996, p. 6, translated in FBIS-SOV-96-212-S, 1 November 1996.

[54] Vladimir Abarinov, *Segodnya*, 13 March 1996, p. 5, translated in Current Digest of the Post-Soviet Press, vol. 48, no. 11, 10 April 1996, p. 12.